TOSEL®
BASIC

 International TOSEL Committee

GRAMMAR 1

CONTENTS

TOSEL® Level Chart TOSEL 단계표

COCOON

아이들이 접할 수 있는 공식 인증 시험의 첫 단계로써, 아이들의 부담을 줄이고 즐겁게 흥미를 유발할 수 있도록 컬러풀한 색상과 디자인으로 시험지를 구성하였습니다.

Pre-STARTER

친숙한 주제에 대한 단어, 짧은 대화, 짧은 문장을 사용한 기본적인 문장표현 능력을 측정합니다.

STARTER

흔히 접할 수 있는 주제와 상황과 관련된 주제에 대한 짧은 대화 및 짧은 문장을 이해하고 일상생활 대화에 참여하며 실질적인 영어 기초 의사소통 능력을 측정합니다.

BASIC

개인 정보와 일상 활동, 미래 계획, 과거의 경험에 대해 구어와 문어의 형태로 의사소통을 할 수 있는 능력을 측정합니다.

JUNIOR

일반적인 주제와 상황을 다루는 회화와 짧은 단락, 실용문, 짧은 연설 등을 이해하고 간단한 일상 대화에 참여하는 능력을 측정합니다.

HIGH JUNIOR

넓은 범위의 사회적, 학문적 주제에서 영어를 유창하고 정확하게, 효과적으로 사용할 수 있는 능력 및 중문과 복잡한 문장을 포함한 다양한 문장구조의 사용 능력을 측정합니다.

ADVANCED

대학 및 대학원에서 요구되는 영어능력과 취업 또는 직업근무환경에 필요한 실용영어 능력을 측정합니다.

COCOON 유치원생 — 영어의 첫 걸음 단계

Pre-STARTER 초등 1,2학년 — 영어를 시작하는 단계

STARTER 초등 3,4학년 — 영어의 밑바탕을 다지는 단계

BASIC 초등 5,6학년 — 영어의 도약 단계

JUNIOR 중학생 — 영어의 실전 단계

HIGH JUNIOR 고등학생 — 영어의 고급화 단계

ADVANCED 대학생,직장인 — 영어의 완성 단계

TOSEL
교재 Series

TOSEL LEVEL	Age	Vocabulary Frequency	Readability Score	교과 과정 연계	Grammar	VOCA	Reading	Listening
Cocoon	K5-K7	500	0-1	Who is he? (국어 1단원 1-1)	There is · There are	150	Picking Pumpkins (Phonics Story)	Phonics
Pre-Starter	P1-P2	700		How old are you? (통합교과 1-1)	be + adjective	300	Me & My Family (Reading series Ch.1)	묘사하기
Starter	P3-P4	1000-2000	1-2	Spring, Summer, Fall, Winter (통합교과 3-1)	Simple Present	800	Ask More Questions (Reading Series Ch.1)	날씨/시간 표현
Basic	P5-P6	3000-4000	3-4	Show and Tell (사회 5-1)	Superlative	1700	Culture (Reading Series Ch.3)	상대방 의견 묻고 답하기
Junior	M1-M2	5000-6000	5-6	중 1, 2 과학, 기술가정	to-infinitive	4000	Humans and Animals (Reading Series Ch.1)	정보 묻고 답하기
High Junior	H1-H3			고등학교 - 체육	2nd Conditional	7000	Health (Reading Series Ch.1)	사건 묘사하기

■ TOSEL의 세분화된 레벨은 각 연령에 맞는 어휘와 읽기 지능 및 교과 과정과의 연계가
가능하도록 설계된 교재들로 효과적인 학습 커리큘럼을 제공합니다.

■ TOSEL의 커리큘럼에 따른 학습은
정확한 레벨링 → 레벨에 적합한 학습 → 영어 능력 인증 시험 TOSEL에서의 공신력 있는 평가를 통해
진단 → 학습 → 평가의 선순환 구조를 실현합니다.

About TOSEL® ——— TOSEL에 대하여

TOSEL은 각급 학교 교과과정과 연령별 인지단계를 고려하여 단계별 난이도와 문항으로
영어 숙달 정도를 측정하는 영어 사용자 중심의 맞춤식 영어능력인증 시험제도입니다.
평가유형에 따른 개인별 장점과 단점을 파악하고, 개인별 영어학습 방향을 제시하는 성적분석자료를 제공하여
영어능력 종합검진 서비스를 제공함으로써 영어 사용자인 소비자와
영어능력 평가를 토대로 영어교육을 담당하는 교사 및 기관 인사관리자인 공급자를
모두 만족시키는 영어능력인증 평가입니다.

TOSEL은 인지적-학문적 언어 사용의 유창성 (Cognitive-Academic Language Proficiency, CALP)과
기본적-개인적 의사소통능력 (Basic Interpersonal Communication Skill, BICS)을
엄밀히 구분하여 수험자의 언어능력을 가장 친밀하게 평가하는 시험입니다.

대상	목적	용도
유아, 초, 중, 고등학생, 대학생 및 직장인 등 성인	한국인의 영어구사능력 증진과 비영어권 국가의 영어 사용자의 영어구사능력 증진	실질적인 영어구사능력 평가 + 입학전형 및 인재선발 등에 활용 및 직무역량별 인재 배치

연혁

2002.02	국제토셀위원회 창설 (수능출제위원역임 전국대학 영어전공교수진 중심)
2004.09	TOSEL 고려대학교 국제어학원 공동인증시험 실시
2006.04	EBS 한국교육방송공사 주관기관 참여
2006.05	민족사관고등학교 입학전형에 반영
2008.12	고려대학교 편입학시험 TOSEL 유형으로 대체
2009.01	서울시 공무원 근무평정에 TOSEL 점수 가산점 부여
2009.01	전국 대부분 외고, 자사고 입학전형에 TOSEL 반영 (한영외국어고등학교, 한일고등학교, 고양외국어고등학교, 과천외국어고등학교, 김포외국어고등학교, 명지외국어고등학교, 부산국제외국어고등학교, 부일외국어 고등학교, 성남외국어고등학교, 인천외국어고등학교, 전북외국어고등학교, 대전외국어고등학교, 청주외국어고등학교, 강원외국어고등학교, 전남외국어고등학교)
2009.12	청심국제중·고등학교 입학전형 TOSEL 반영
2009.12	한국외국어교육학회, 팬코리아영어교육학회, 한국음성학회, 한국응용언어학회 TOSEL 인증
2010.03	고려대학교, TOSEL 출제기관 및 공동 인증기관으로 참여
2010.07	경찰청 공무원 임용 TOSEL 성적 가산점 부여
2014.04	전국 200개 초등학교 단체 응시 실시
2017.03	중앙일보 주관기관 참여
2018.11	관공서, 대기업 등 100여 개 기관에서 TOSEL 반영
2019.06	미얀마 TOSEL 도입 발족식 베트남 TOSEL 도입 협약식
2019.11	2020학년도 고려대학교 편입학전형 반영
2020.04	국토교통부 국가자격시험 TOSEL 반영
2021.07	소방청 간부후보생 선발시험 TOSEL 반영

About **TOSEL**® ——— **TOSEL에 대하여**

What's TOSEL?

"Test of Skills in the English Language"

TOSEL은 비영어권 국가의 영어 사용자를 대상으로 영어구사능력을 측정하여
그 결과를 공식 인증하는 영어능력인증 시험제도입니다.

영어 사용자 중심의 맞춤식 영어능력 인증 시험제도

맞춤식 평가

**획일적인 평가에서
세분화된 평가로의 전환**

TOSEL은 응시자의 연령별
인지단계에 따라 별도의 문항과 난이도를
적용하여 평가함으로써 평가의
목적과 용도에 적합한 평가 시스템을
구축하였습니다.

공정성과 신뢰성 확보

국제토셀위원회의 역할

TOSEL은 고려대학교가 출제 및 인증기관
으로 참여하였고 대학입학수학능력시험 출
제위원 교수들이
중심이 된 국제토셀위원회가 주관하여
사회적 공정성과 신뢰성을 확보한
평가 제도입니다.

수입대체 효과

외화유출 차단 및 국위선양

TOSEL은 해외시험응시로 인한 외화의 유
출을 막는 수입대체의 효과를 기대할 수 있
습니다. TOSEL의 문항과 시험제도는 비영
어권 국가에 수출하여 국위선양에
기여하고 있습니다.

Why TOSEL® ——— 왜 TOSEL인가

01 학교 시험 폐지

일선 학교에서 중간, 기말고사 폐지로 인해 객관적인 영어 평가 제도의 부재가 우려됩니다. 그러나 전국단위로 연간 4번 시행되는 TOSEL 평가시험을 통해 학생들은 정확한 역량과 체계적인 학습방향을 꾸준히 진단받을 수 있습니다.

02 연령별/단계별 대비로 영어학습 점검

TOSEL은 응시자의 연령별 인지단계 및 영어 학습 단계에 따라 총 7단계로 구성되었습니다. 각 단계에 알맞은 문항유형과 난이도를 적용해 모든 연령 및 학습 과정에 맞추어 가장 효율적으로 영어실력을 평가할 수 있도록 개발된 영어시험입니다.

03 학교내신성적 향상

TOSEL은 학년별 교과과정과 연계하여 학교에서 배우는 내용을 학습하고 평가할 수 있도록 문항 및 주제를 구성하여 내신영어 향상을 위한 최적의 솔루션을 제공합니다.

04 수능대비 직결

유아, 초, 중등시절 어렵지 않고 즐겁게 학습해 온 영어이지만, 수능시험준비를 위해 접하는 영어의 문항 및 유형 난이도에 주춤하게 됩니다. 이를 대비하기 위해 TOSEL은 유아부터 성인까지 점진적인 학습을 통해 수능대비를 자연적으로 해나갈 수 있습니다.

05 진학과 취업에 대비한 필수 스펙관리

개인별 '학업성취기록부' 발급을 통해 영어학업성취이력을 꾸준히 기록한 영어학습 포트폴리오를 제공하여 영어학습 이력을 관리할 수 있습니다.

06 자기소개서에 토셀 기재

개별적인 진로 적성 Report를 제공하여 진로를 파악하고 자기소개서 작성시 적극적으로 활용할 수 있는 객관적인 자료를 제공합니다.

07 영어학습 동기부여

시험실시 후 응시자 모두에게 수여되는 인증서는 영어학습에 대한 자신감과 성취감을 고취시키고 동기를 부여합니다.

08 AI 분석 영어학습 솔루션

국내외 15,000여 개 학교·학원 단체 응시인원 중 엄선한 100만 명 이상의 실제 TOSEL 성적 데이터를 기반으로 영어인증시험 제도 중 세계 최초로 인공지능이 분석한 개인별 AI 정밀 진단 성적표를 제공합니다. 최첨단 AI 정밀진단 성적표는 최적의 영어 학습 솔루션을 제시하여 영어 학습에 소요되는 시간과 노력을 획기적으로 절감해줍니다.

09 명예의 전당, 우수협력기관 지정

우수교육기관은 'TOSEL 우수 협력 기관'에 지정되고, 각 시/도별, 최고득점자를 명예의 전당에 등재합니다.

Evaluation ———— 평가

평가의 기본원칙

TOSEL은 PBT(Paper Based Test)를 통하여 간접평가와 직접평가를 모두 시행합니다.

TOSEL은 언어의 네 가지 요소인 읽기, 듣기, 말하기, 쓰기 영역을 모두 평가합니다.

문자언어
음성언어

읽기능력
듣기능력

+

쓰기능력
말하기능력

↓

대한민국 대표 영어능력 인증 시험제도

TOSEL®

Reading 읽기	모든 레벨의 읽기 영역은 직접 평가 방식으로 측정합니다.
Listening 듣기	모든 레벨의 듣기 영역은 직접 평가 방식으로 측정합니다.
Writing 쓰기	모든 레벨의 쓰기 영역은 간접 평가 방식으로 측정합니다.
Speaking 말하기	모든 레벨의 말하기 영역은 간접 평가 방식으로 측정합니다.

TOSEL은 연령별 인지단계를 고려하여 아래와 같이 7단계로 나누어 평가합니다.

❶ 단계	**TOSEL® COCOON**	**5~7세의 미취학 아동**
❷ 단계	**TOSEL® Pre-STARTER**	**초등학교 1~2학년**
❸ 단계	**TOSEL® STARTER**	**초등학교 3~4학년**
❹ 단계	**TOSEL® BASIC**	**초등학교 5~6학년**
❺ 단계	**TOSEL® JUNIOR**	**중학생**
❻ 단계	**TOSEL® HIGH JUNIOR**	**고등학생**
❼ 단계	**TOSEL® ADVANCED**	**대학생 및 성인**

Grade Report ——————— 성적표 및 인증서

개인 AI 정밀진단 성적표

십 수년간 전국단위 정기시험으로 축적된 빅데이터를 교육공학적으로 분석·활용하여 산출한 개인별 성적자료

정확한 영어능력진단 / 섹션별·파트별 영어능력 및 균형 진단 / 명예의 전당 등재 여부 / 온라인 최적화된 개인별 상세
성적자료를 위한 QR코드 / 응시지역, 동일학년, 전국에서의 학생의 위치

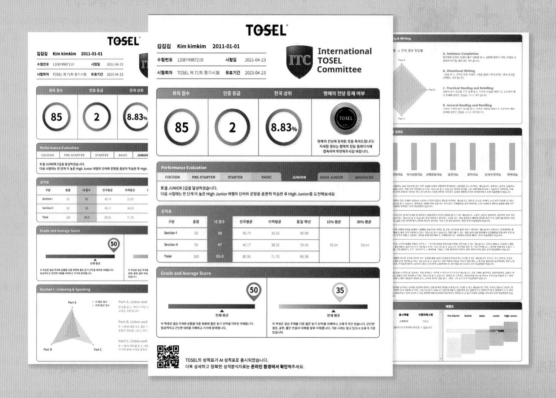

단체 및 기관 응시자 AI 통계 분석 자료

십 수년간 전국단위 정기시험으로 **축적된 빅데이터를**
교육공학적으로 분석·활용하여 산출한 응시자 통계 분석 자료

- 단체 내 레벨별 평균성적추이, LR평균 점수, 표준편차 파악
- 타 지역 내 다른 단체와의 점수 종합 비교 / 단체 내 레벨별
  학생분포 파악
- 동일 지역 내 다른 단체 레벨별 응시자의 평균 나이 비교
- 동일 지역 내 다른 단체 명예의 전당 등재 인원 수 비교
- 동일 지역 내 다른 단체 최고점자의 최고 점수 비교
- 동일 지역 내 다른 응시자들의 수 비교

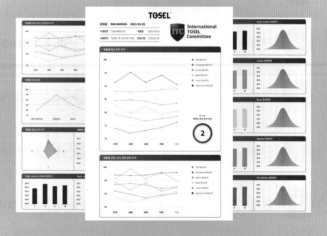

'토셀 명예의 전당' 등재

특별시, 광역시, 도 별 **1등 선발**
(7개시 9개도 **1등 선발**)

*홈페이지 로그인 – 시험결과 – 명예의 전당에서
 해당자 등재 증명서 출력 가능

'학업성취기록부'에 토셀 인증등급 기재

개인별 **'학업성취기록부' 평생 발급**
진학과 취업을 대비한 **필수 스펙관리**

인증서

대한민국 초,중,고등학생의 영어숙달능력 평가 결과 공식인증

고려대학교 인증획득 (2010. 03)   팬코리아영어교육학회 인증획득 (2009. 10)   한국응용언어학회 인증획득 (2009. 11)
한국외국어교육학회 인증획득 (2009. 12)   한국음성학회 인증획득 (2009. 12)

Grammar Series ——— 특장점

TOSEL 시험을 기준으로 빈출 지표를 활용한 문법 선정 및 예문과 문제 구성

TOSEL 시험 활용

- ■ 실제 TOSEL 시험에 출제된 빈출 문항을 기준으로 단계별 학습을 위한 문법 선정
- ■ 실제 TOSEL 시험에 활용된 문장을 사용하여 예문과 문제를 구성
- ■ 문법 학습 이외에 TOSEL 기출 문제 풀이를 통해서 TOSEL 및 실전 영어 시험 대비 학습

세분화된 레벨링

20년 간 대한민국 영어 평가 기관으로서

연간 4회 전국적으로 실시되는 정기시험에서

축적된 성적 데이터를 기반으로

정확하고 세분화된 레벨링을 통한

영어 학습 콘텐츠 개발

언어의 4대 영역 균형 학습 + 평가

1. TOSEL 평가: 학생의 영어 능력을 정확하게 평가

2. 결과 분석 및 진단: 시험 점수와 결과를 분석하여 학생의 강점, 취약점, 학습자 특성 능늘 객관적으로 진단

3. 학습 방향 제시: 객관적 진단 데이터를 기반으로 학습자 특성에 맞는 학습 방향 제시 및 목표 설정

4. 학습: 제시된 방향과 목표에 따라 학생에게 적합한 문법 학습법 소개 및 영어의 체계와 구조 이해

5. 학습 목표 달성: 학습 후 다시 평가를 통해 목표 달성 여부 확인 및 성장을 위한 다음 학습 목표 설정

Grammar Series —————— Level

TOSEL의 Grammar Series는 레벨에 맞게 단계적으로
문법을 학습할 수 있도록 구성되어 있습니다.

Pre-Starter	Starter	Basic	Junior	High Junior

■ 그림을 활용하여 문법에 대한 이해도 향상

■ 다양한 활동을 통해 문법 반복 학습 유도

■ TOSEL 기출 문제 연습을 통한 실전 대비

■ TOSEL 기출의 빈도수를 활용한 문법 선정으로 효율적 학습

■ 실제 TOSEL 지문의 예문을 활용한 실용적 학습 제공

■ TOSEL 기출 문제 연습을 통한 실전 대비

최신 수능 출제
문법을 포함하여
수능 대비 가능

1시간 학습 Guideline

01 Unit Intro
2분

■ 초등 교육과정에서 익혀야 하는 문법과 단어를 중심으로 단원의 문법에 대해 미리 생각해보기

02 개념
15분

■ 문법 개념을 익히고 예문을 통해 문법이 어떻게 적용되는지 익히기

05 Sentence Completion
10분

■ Unit에서 배운 문법을 활용하여 문제 해결하기

■ 틀린 문제에 대해서는 해당 Unit에서 복습하도록 지도하기

06 Writing Activity
3분

■ 빈도수가 높은 주요 단어 위주로 writing activity를 추가하여 쓰기 학습 지도

■ 단어를 소리 내어 읽으며, 점선을 따라 스펠링을 쓰도록 지도하기

03
 Activity 1 / Activity 2

■ 배운 문법을 활용하여 문제 해결하기

■ 연결하기, OX 문제, 빈칸 채우기 등
다양한 방법으로 문법 적용하기

04
Exercise 1 / Exercise 2

■ 다양한 Exercise 활동을 하며 혼동하기 쉬운
문법 학습

07
Unit Review

■ 빈칸을 채우는 형태로 구성하여 수업 시간 후
복습에 용이하게 구성

■ 배운 문법을 직접 활용하여 수업 시간 후
복습에 용이하게 구성

08
TOSEL 실전문제

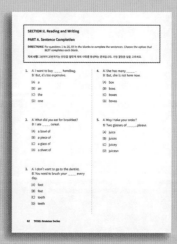

■ 실제 TOSEL 기출 문제를 통한 실전 대비 학습

■ 실제 시험 시간과 유사하게 풀이할 수 있도록 지도하기

■ 틀린 문제에 대해서는 해당 단원에서 복습하도록 지도하기

PreStarter/Starter/Basic Syllabus

PreStarter		Basic		2015 개정 초등 영어 언어형식
Chapter	Unit	Chapter	Unit	
I. 명사: 명사는 이름이야	1 셀 수 있는 명사	I. 명사	1 셀 수 있는 명사 앞에 붙는 관사 the/a/an	A boy/The **boy**/The (two) boys ran in the park. **The** store is closed.
	2 셀 수 있는 명사 앞에 붙는 관사 a/an		2 셀 수 없는 명사를 측정하는 단위	**Water** is very important for life. **Kate** is from **London**.
	3 셀 수 없는 명사		3 규칙 복수명사	The **two boys** ran in the park.
	4 명사의 복수형		4 불규칙 복수명사	
II. 대명사: 명사를 대신하는 대명사	1 주격 대명사	II. 대명사	1 단수대명사의 격	**She** is a teacher, and **he**'s a scientist. I like **your** glasses. What about **mine**?
	2 소유격 대명사		2 복수대명사의 격	**They**'re really delicious. **We** are very glad to hear from him.
	3 목적격 대명사		3 1, 2인칭 대명사의 활용	**I** like math, but Susan doesn't like it. He will help **you**.
	4 지시대명사		4 3인칭 대명사의 활용	Which do you like better, **this** or **that**? **These** are apples, and **those** are tomatoes. **That** dog is smart. **These/Those** books are really large.
III. 형용사: 명사&대명사를 꾸미는 형용사	1 형용사의 명사수식	III. 동사	1 동사의 기본시제	He **walks** to school every day. We **played** soccer yesterday. She **is going to** visit her grandparents next week. He **is sleeping** now. I **will visit** America next year.
	2 형용사의 대명사수식		2 동사의 불규칙 과거형	
	3 숫자와 시간		3 헷갈리기 쉬운 동사	**It's half past four**. **What time** is it?
				I **don't** like snakes. We **didn't** enjoy the movie very much.
	4 지시형용사		4 조동사	She **can** play the violin. Tom **won't** be at the meeting tomorrow. I **will** visit America next year. You **may** leave now.

Junior Syllabus

Junior

Chapter	Unit	2015 개정 중등 영어 언어형식
I. 8품사 (1)	1 명사	She lived in the **woods** when she was kid. Thank you for your **kindness**.
	2 대명사	I have **three books**. **One** is mine. **The others** are yours. **The chocolate cookie** is sweet. I'm going to have **another one**.
	3 형용사	Something **strange** happened last night.
	4 감탄사	**How** beautiful she is! **What** a player!
II 8품사 (2)	1 동사	**Mathematics** is my favorite subject. **Each** boy admires his teacher. **Both** the teacher **and** the students enjoyed the class. You can have **either** tea or coffee. It is **not only** beautiful **but (also)** useful.
	2 부사	
	3 전치사	
	4 접속사	I may stop by tomorrow **or** just phone you. Both the teacher **and** the students enjoyed the class.
III. 문장의 구조	1 문장성분의 기초	You can **put the dish on the table**. He **gave me a present**. They **elected him president**.
	2 문장의 형식	
	3 평서문의 전환	
	4 의문문의 비교	**Have you** finished your homework yet? This is your book, **isn't it**?
IV. 문장의 시제	1 단순시제	I **will be** able to help you get to the party tonight. **Are you going** to take the last train?
	2 진행시제	**I'm thinking** about the problem. I **was studying** when John called me.
	3 현재완료	The bakery **has been** open since 1960. He **has attended** the club meetings regularly.
	4 시간을 나타내는 접속사	**Since** he left this morning, I haven't seen him. **When** we arrived, she was talking on the phone.
V. to부정사와 동명사	1 to부정사	**To see** is **to belive**. Chris was glad **to hear the news**.
	2 동명사	We **enjoy swimming** in the pool. Life is **worth living**. I'm interested in **watching horror movies**.
	3 to부정사와 동명사 비교	
	4 의미상주어	It is difficult **for me to speak French**. It was kind **of you to help us**.
VI. 비교급과 최상급	1 비교급과 최상급의 규칙 변화	They've got **more/less** money **than** they need. A car is **much more** expensive **than** a motorbike.
	2 비교급과 최상급의 불규칙 변화	
	3 원급의 비교	You can run **as fast as** Billy can. She is old, but she is not **as old as** he (is).
	4 최상급의 비교	Cindy is **the shortest** of the three. It is **the most interesting** speech I've ever heard.

High Junior Syllabus

High Junior		2015 개정 중등 영어 언어형식
Chapter	**Unit**	
I. 문장의 형성	1 8품사와 문장 성분	**The audience** is/are enjoying the show. I'd like to **write a diary**, but I'm too busy to do so. He**'s being** very rude. We **are hoping** you will be with us.
	2 문장의 형식	
	3 문장의 배열	I think **(that)** he is a good actor. **Although/Though** it was cold, I went swimming.
	4 문장의 강조	The weather was **so** nice **that** we went hiking. **It was Justin who/that** told me the truth.
II 부정사와 동명사	1 원형부정사	You shouldn't **let** him **go** there again. I **heard** the children **sing/singing**.
	2 to부정사	He seemed **to have been ill (for some time)**. Bill promised Jane **to work out with her**. I remembered **John/John's coming** late for class. It goes without **saying that time is money**. There is no use **crying over the spilt milk**.
	3 동명사	
	4 to부정사와 동명사구	
III. 분사	1 현재분사	At the station I met a lady **carrying a large umbrella**. **With the night coming**, stars began to shine in the sky.
	2 과거분사	Wallets **found on the street** must be reported to the police.
	3 분사구문	**Walking along the street,** I met an old friend. **Having seen that movie before,** I wanted to see it again.
	4 독립분사구문	**Joshua returning home,** the puppy ran toward him. **Frankly speaking,** I failed the test.
IV. 수동태	1 수동태의 형성	The building **was built** in 1880. I **was made** to clean the room. Nolan **was seen** to enter the building. The monkey **has been raised** by human parents for years. Cooper **will be invited** to today's meeting. The information superhighway **will have been introduced** to everyone by 2015.
	2 수동태와 능동태의 전환	
	3 수동태와 전치사의 사용	
	4 주의해야 할 수동태 용법	
V. 관계대명사와 관계부사	1 관계대명사의 사용	The girl **who is playing the piano** is called Ann. This is the book **(that) I bought yesterday**.
	2 관계대명사와 선행사	Please tell me **what happened**.
	3 관계대명사의 생략	This is **why** we have to study English grammar.
	4 관계부사	The town **in which I was born** is very small. That's just **how he talks**, always serious about his work.
VI. 가정법	1 가정법 현재와 과거	**If it were not for you, I would** be lonely.
	2 가정법 과거완료	**Had** I had enough money, I **would have bought** a cell phone. **Without/But for** your advice, I **would have** failed.
	3 혼합가정법	I **wish** I **had learned** swimming last summer. He acts **as if** he **had been** there.
	4 특수가정법	I'd **rather** we **had** dinner now. **Provided that/As long as** they had plenty to eat, the crew **seemed** to be happy.

UNIT 03

규칙 복수명사

단수명사	셀 수 있는 명사가 하나일 때
복수명사	-(e)s 셀 수 있는 명사가 여러 개일 때

way	방법	leaf	잎
seat	자리	stomach	위, 복부, 배
brush	붓	photo	사진
potato	감자	chief	우두머리, 추장, 족장
content	내용	factory	공장

❶ 어미에 '-s'를 붙이는 경우

> ❶ 대부분의 명사
>
> I love your cups.
>
> ❷ 어미가 '모음+y'인 경우
>
> There are two ways.
>
> ❸ 어미가 '모음+o'인 경우
>
> Most children like zoos.

❷ 어미에 '-es'를 붙이는 경우

어미에 '-es'를 붙이는 경우

> ❶ 어미가 '-s, -sh, -ch, -x' 등인 경우
>
> There are big buses over there.
>
> Where are their brushes?
>
> I know many churches.
>
> Let's open the boxes.
>
> ❷ 어미가 '자음 + o'인 경우
>
> He digs potatoes every year.

어미를 고치고 '-es'를 붙이는 경우

> ❶ 어미가 '자음 + y'인 경우 y를 i로 고치고 '-es' 붙임
>
> She likes her grandmother's old stories.
>
> ❷ 어미가 '-f(e)'인 경우 'f(e)'를 v로 고치고 '-es' 붙임
>
> He sees the leaves.
>
> She owns her knives.

❸ 규칙 복수명사의 예외

① 어미 '-ch'가 [k]로 발음되는 경우

The patients suffer from upset **stomach**s.

② 특정 단어들

Alex takes many **photo**s.

Many tribes admire their **chief**s.

③ 단수형과 복수형의 의미가 다른 경우

Jenny seems **content** with the **content**s.

④ 복수형으로 쓰이지만 항상 단수 취급하는 경우

Peter teaches **mathematic**s at the school.

Activity 1

보기 안의 단어들을 적절한 복수명사 항목에 분류해보세요.

보기	tomato church company box hand
	glass knife cup wife party

'-s'를 붙이는 경우	y를 i로 고치고 '-es'를 붙이는 경우
'-es'를 붙이는 경우	f(e)를 v로 고치고 '-es'를 붙이는 경우

Activity 2

다음 그림 안에서 복수형 어미가 -es인 물건을 모두 찾으세요.

물건   sofa   plant   picture   book   table   knife   dish   box

Exercise 1

알맞은 단어를 골라 문장을 완성하세요.

❶ I have many **cardes / cards** .

❷ We will go around the **factories / factoryes** .

❸ There are two **seates / seats** in the row.

❹ In May, our village has a lot of **festivals / festivales** .

❺ My mother bought three **dishes / disies** .

Exercise 2

빈칸에 알맞은 복수형 단어를 쓰세요.

❶ _____ stop in the bus station.
버스들은 버스 정류장에서 멈춘다.

❷ Children like small _____ .
아이들은 작은 동물들을 좋아한다.

❸ The _____ played soccer after school.
소년들은 방과 후에 축구를 했다.

❹ The _____ hide in the bush.
늑대들은 수풀에 몸을 숨겼다.

❺ There are many _____ on his farm.
그의 농장에는 많은 토마토들이 있다.

Sentence Completion

1 A: How much are two ⬚⬚⬚⬚⬚ ?

  B: Each one is 5 dollars.

(A) ticket

(B) tickies

(C) tickets

(D) ticketes

2 A: There are many ⬚⬚⬚⬚⬚ .

  B: I like the white one.

(A) piano

(B) pianos

(C) pianies

(D) pianoes

3 A: What are you doing?

  B: I'm sweeping the ⬚⬚⬚⬚⬚ .

(A) leaf

(B) leafs

(C) leafes

(D) leaves

4 A: Two ⬚⬚⬚⬚⬚ are on the tree.

  B: They are picking a banana.

(A) monkey

(B) monkeys

(C) monkeies

(D) monkeyes

5 A: There are many ⬚⬚⬚⬚⬚
  in my room.

  B: Clean your room first.

(A) bug

(B) bugs

(C) buies

(D) buges

6 A: The tree has lots of _____ .

B: It is an old tree.

(A) branch

(B) branchs

(C) brancies

(D) branches

9 A: There are many _____

in the cage.

B: I want to see them closely.

(A) fox

(B) foxs

(C) foxes

(D) foxen

7 A: The players look tired.

B: They had many _____ before.

(A) match

(B) matchs

(C) matcies

(D) matches

10 A: There are some _____

orbiting the sun.

B: It's an interesting story.

(A) planet

(B) planets

(C) plannis

(D) planetes

8 A: She likes _____ .

B: Oh, I like it too.

(A) noodles

(B) noodlies

(C) noodlese

(D) noodlves

1 **way**
방법

way

2 **seat**
자리

seat

3 **brush**
붓

brush

4 **potato**
감자

potato

5 **content**
내용

content

6 **leaf**
잎

leaf

7 **stomach**
위, 복부, 배

stomach

8 **photo**
사진

photo

9 **chief**
우두머리, 추장, 족장

chief

10 **factory**
공장

factory

✎ Unit Review

배운 내용 스스로 정리해보기

❶ 어미에 '-s'를 붙이는 경우

어미에 '-s'를 붙이는 경우는 ❶ 대부분의 명사, ❷   인 경우, ❸   인 경우이다.

예시문장 써보기

❶ day의 복수형 사용하기

➜ _____

❷ bamboo의 복수형 사용하기

➜ _____

❷ 어미에 '-es'를 붙이는 경우

예시문장 써보기

❶ watch의 복수형 사용하기

➜ _____

❷ lady의 복수형 사용하기

➜ _____

❸ 규칙 복수명사의 예외

예시문장 써보기

❶ stomach의 복수형 사용하기

➜ _____

❷ physics의 복수형 사용하기

➜ _____

UNIT 04

—

불규칙 복수명사

복수명사

규칙 복수명사	-(e)s 어미에 따라 '-s' 또는 '-es'를 붙여 복수형 형성
불규칙 복수명사	1. 단수명사와 형태가 같은 경우 2. 모음이 변화하는 경우 3. 어미에 -(r)en이 붙는 경우 4. 라틴어·그리스어에서 유래한 경우

sheep	양	tooth	치아
salmon	연어	ox	황소
goose	거위	deer	사슴
children	아이들	stimulus	자극제
person	사람	crisis	위기

UNIT **4** 불규칙 복수명사

❶ 단수와 복수의 형태가 같은 경우

A sheep leads many sheep.

The deer looks different from other deer.

Three salmon are following **a** salmon.

Chinese usually like red, but my Chinese friend hates the color.

❷ 단수와 복수의 형태가 전혀 다른 경우

모음이 변하는 경우

❶ a too**th ➜ t**ee**th, a f**oo**t ➜ f**ee**t, a g**oo**se ➜ g**ee**se**

You need to brush your **t**ee**th** every day.

He washes his **f**ee**t** by himself.

Look! The g**ee**se swim to us.

❷ a ma**n ➜ m**e**n, a wom**a**n ➜ wom**e**n**

The two **m**e**n** are very different.

Three **wom**e**n** are in Kate's house.

❸ a pe**rson ➜ p**eople**, a m**ouse **➜ m**ice

We live with a lot of **p**eople.

Cats always chase **m**ice.

어미에 -(r)en이 붙는 경우

❶ 어미에 -en이 붙는 경우: an ox ➜ oxen

What do the **ox**en look like?

❷ 어미에 -ren이 붙는 경우: a child ➜ children

Today is **Child**ren's Day.

라틴어와 그리스에서 유래한 경우

① **라틴어에서 유래: a stimul**us ➜ **stimul**i**, a med**ium ➜ **medi**a

Dogs respond to the **stimul**i.

② **그리스어에서 유래: cris**is ➜ **cris**es**, phenomen**on ➜ **phenomen**a

Crises become opportunities.

She studies natural **phenomen**a.

Activity 1

다음 명사의 복수형을 알맞게 연결해보세요.

sheep	●	●	media
man	●	●	sheep
tooth	●	●	oxen
medium	●	●	men
ox	●	●	teeth

Activity 2

다음 그림에서 단수와 복수의 형태가 같은 동물에 O표 하고 각 단어의 단수형과 복수형을 차례로 쓰세요.

❶ _____ ➜ _____

❷ _____ ➜ _____

❸ _____ ➜ _____

Exercise 1

알맞은 단어를 골라 문장을 완성하세요.

❶ There are many **children / child** in the playground.

❷ Some **goose / geese** swim in the pond.

❸ I saw some **mouse / mice** in the kitchen.

❹ A herd of **deer / deers** are running in the plain.

❺ Both **women / woman** are American.

Exercise 2

빈칸에 알맞은 복수형 단어를 쓰세요.

❶ He has a lot of _____ on his ranch.
그는 그의 목장에 많은 황소들을 가지고 있다.

❷ Check your _____ at the dentist.
치과에서 너의 치아들을 검사해봐라.

❸ They responded the same to the _____.
그들은 그 자극들에 동일한 반응을 보였다.

❹ The _____ are swimming against a river.
연어들이 강을 거슬러 헤엄치는 중이다.

❺ There are some _____ in the lobby.
로비에 몇몇 사람들이 있다.

Sentence Completion

1 A: Some _____ are in the river.

B: Oh, I want to see them.

(A) salmon

(B) a salmon

(C) salmons

(D) an salmon

2 A: Clean your hands and _____ first.

B: Ok, I will.

(A) feet

(B) foot

(C) feets

(D) foots

3 A: There were some _____ in the morning.

B: What happened?

(A) crisis

(B) crises

(C) crisesn

(D) crisises

4 A: We can get lots of _____ in the library.

B: I'll check the history section.

(A) data

(B) datas

(C) datum

(D) datums

5 A: Look at those _____.

B: They are so cute.

(A) sheep

(B) sheeps

(C) shepen

(D) a sheep

6 A: We can see some _____ in the desert.

B: How can they live there?

(A) cacti

(B) cactus

(C) cactum

(D) cactues

7 A: It's hard to read these _____ .

B: Never mind. It's for university students.

(A) thesis

(B) theses

(C) thesisen

(D) thesesen

8 A: She is one of the influential _____ these days.

B: I heard about her.

(A) man

(B) woman

(C) women

(D) womans

9 A: Some _____ are swimming.

B: They flock together.

(A) geese

(B) goose

(C) geeses

(D) gooses

10 A: There are so many _____ in front of the ticket office.

B: We should have gone earlier.

(A) person

(B) people

(C) peoples

(D) persons

1 **sheep**
양

sheep

2 **salmon**
연어

salmon

3 **goose**
거위

goose

4 **children**
아이들

children

5 **person**
사람

person

6 tooth

치아

tooth

7 ox

황소

ox

8 deer

사슴

deer

9 stimulus

자극제

stimulus

10 crisis

위기

crisis

Unit Review

배운 내용 스스로 정리해보기

❶ 단수와 복수의 형태가 같은 경우

예시문장 써보기

① sheep의 복수형 사용하기

→ _____

② fish의 복수형 사용하기

→ _____

❷ 단수와 복수의 형태가 전혀 다른 경우

예시문장 써보기

① tooth의 복수형 사용하기

→ _____

② man의 복수형 사용하기

→ _____

③ person의 복수형 사용하기

→ _____

④ child의 복수형 사용하기

→ _____

⑤ phenomenon의 복수형 사용하기

→ _____

TOSEL 실전문제 ①

PART A. Sentence Completion

DIRECTIONS: For questions 1 to 20, fill in the blanks to complete the sentences. Choose the option that BEST completes each blank.

지시 사항: 1번부터 20번까지는 빈칸을 알맞게 채워 대화를 완성하는 문제입니다. 가장 알맞은 답을 고르세요.

1. A: I want to buy _____ handbag.
    B: But, it's too expensive.

    (A) a

    (B) an

    (C) the

    (D) one

2. A: What did you eat for breakfast?
    B: I ate _____ cereal.

    (A) a bowl of

    (B) a piece of

    (C) a glass of

    (D) a sheet of

3. A: I don't want to go to the dentist.
    B: You need to brush your _____ every day.

    (A) foot

    (B) feet

    (C) tooth

    (D) teeth

4. A: She has many _____ .
    B: But, she is not here now.

    (A) box

    (B) boxs

    (C) boxes

    (D) boves

5. A: May I take your order?
    B: Two glasses of _____, please.

    (A) juice

    (B) juices

    (C) juicey

    (D) juicesn

6. A: Look at those _____.
   B: They look fresh. I would like to buy some.

   (A) salmon

   (B) salmons

   (C) a salmon

   (D) an salmon

7. A: Which pencil is yours?
   B: _____ red one on the book.

   (A) A

   (B) An

   (C) The

   (D) One

8. A: Let's set up the table.
   B: Ok. We need two more _____.

   (A) knife

   (B) knifes

   (C) knives

   (D) a knife

9. A: There are so many _____ here!
   B: It is a famous show.

   (A) person

   (B) people

   (C) a person

   (D) a people

10. A: Help yourself.
    B: I'll take _____ pizza.

    (A) a bar of

    (B) a bars of

    (C) a slice of

    (D) a slices of

11. A: Did you watch _____ game yesterday?
B: Yes, I did. It was fun.

(A) a

(B) an

(C) the

(D) one

14. A: I want to be _____ doctor.
B: Then, you should study a lot.

(A) a

(B) an

(C) the

(D) that

12. A: The _____ are her friends.
B: I know them.

(A) woman

(B) women

(C) womans

(D) womens

15. A: She cut _____ cake.
B: It looks delicious.

(A) a

(B) a slice of

(C) a glass of

(D) a pound of

13. A: He is taking many _____.
B: He likes it very much.

(A) photo

(B) photos

(C) photies

(D) photoes

16. A: There are many _____ in the park.
    B: It's so crowded.

    (A) person

    (B) people

    (C) peoples

    (D) persons

19. A: He has a lot of _____ in his farm.
    B: I want to see them.

    (A) sheep

    (B) sheeps

    (C) sheepen

    (D) sheepes

17. A: It's already fall.
    B: We should sweep the _____.

    (A) leaf

    (B) leafs

    (C) leafes

    (D) leaves

20. A: I want to buy a new cup.
    B: But, you already have many _____.

    (A) cup

    (B) cups

    (C) cupes

    (D) a glass of cups

18. A: The show will begin in _____ hour.
    B: I can't wait for it.

    (A) a

    (B) an

    (C) the

    (D) this

CHAPTER 02

II. 대명사

UNIT 01

—

단수 대명사의 격

인칭대명사

단수 주격	I, you, he, she, it
단수 소유격	my, your, his, her, its
단수 목적격	me, you, him, her, it

name	이름	cute	귀여운
country	국가, 시골	sunflower	해바라기
famous	유명한	present	선물
health	건강	theater	극장
label	표, 상표	blame	비난하다

❶ 단수대명사 표

단수 대명사의 표는 다음과 같다.

		주격	소유격	목적격	소유대명사
단수	1인칭	I	my	me	mine
	2인칭	you	your	you	yours
	3인칭	he	his	him	his
		she	her	her	hers
		it	its	it	-

❷ 주격

주격 대명사는 '~은/는/이/가'로 해석한다.

I have two brothers.

You are very tall.

He is famous in his country.

We like a cat. It is cute.

TIP 비인칭주어 **it**

● 날씨·시간·거리 등을 나타내며 '그것'이라고 해석하지 않음.
　예) 날씨: It is raining.
　　　시간: It is 2 o'clock.
　　　거리: How far is it from here?

❸ 소유격

소유격 대명사는 '~의'로 해석한다.

He borrowed my eraser.

I envy your health.

She admires her teacher.

Its name is sunflower.

❹ 목적격

목적격 대명사는 '~을/를, ~에게'로 해석한다.

My mom calls me.
I love you so much.
He believes her.
I observe it every day.

❺ 소유대명사

소유대명사는 '소유격 + 명사'로 '~의 것'으로 해석한다.

The book is mine.
This pen is yours.
The shirt is his.

Activity 1

다음 주격 대명사를 알맞은 소유격, 목적격, 소유대명사에 연결해보세요.

I		her
You		Its
He		mine
She		his
It		Yours

Activity 2

빙고 칸을 채우고 같은 격 (주격, 소유격, 목적격)을 이어 3빙고를 만들어주세요.

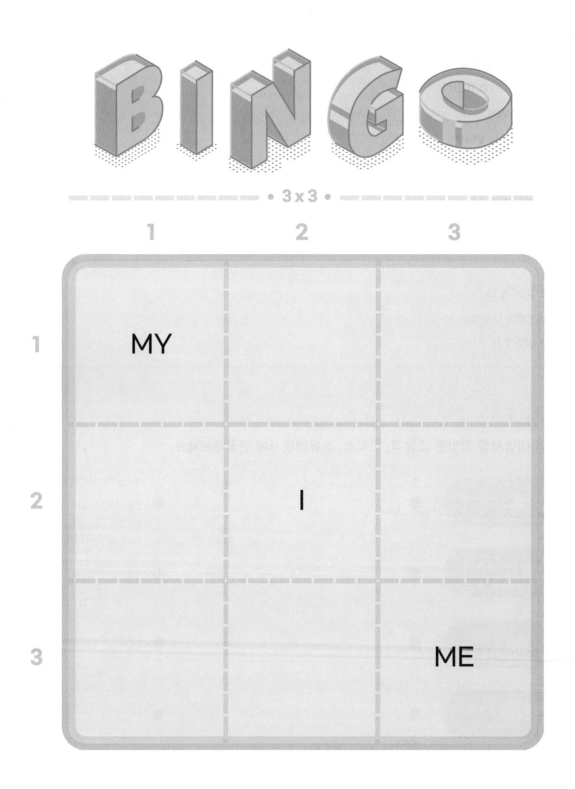

BINGO

• 3 x 3 •

	1	2	3
1	MY		
2		I	
3			ME

Exercise 1

알맞은 단어를 골라 문장을 완성하세요.

❶ **You / Your** dress is so nice.

❷ She helped **he / him** study.

❸ The blue one is **my / mine** .

❹ I want to see **it / its** after school.

❺ **Her / Hers** sweater is there.

Exercise 2

빈칸에 알맞은 복수형 단어를 쓰세요.

❶ He is _____ brother.
그는 그녀의 남동생이다.

❷ The present is for _____ .
그 선물은 그를 위한 것이다.

❸ The bag is _____ .
그 가방은 너의 것이다.

❹ _____ color is red.
그것의 색깔은 빨간색이다.

❺ He asked _____ to go to the theater.
그는 그녀에게 영화관에 가자고 말했다.

Sentence Completion

1. A: What is _____ name?
   B: His name is Ronaldo.

   (A) he
   (B) his
   (C) him
   (D) hime

2. A: _____ blames herself.
   B: I'm worried about her.

   (A) He
   (B) She
   (C) Her
   (D) Hers

3. A: I met _____ yesterday.
   B: Is he okay?

   (A) he
   (B) she
   (C) him
   (D) hers

4. A: The money is _____.
   B: Where did you lose the money?

   (A) I
   (B) my
   (C) me
   (D) mine

5. A: I can make _____.
   B: I'll help you too.

   (A) it
   (B) its
   (C) her
   (D) your

6 A: _____ label is on the table.

B: Thanks, I forgot it.

(A) I

(B) You

(C) Your

(D) Yours

9 A: They always bite _____ .

B: Doesn't it hurt?

(A) I

(B) we

(C) our

(D) me

7 A: Is this book _____ ?

B: No, It's not mine.

(A) you

(B) your

(C) yours

(D) youres

10 A: The clay helps _____ exercise his hand muscles.

B: I hope he gets better soon.

(A) he

(B) his

(C) him

(D) hiss

8 A: Relax _____ body and don't be afraid.

B: Ok, give me a second.

(A) my

(B) you

(C) your

(D) yours

1 name

name

이름

2 country

country

국가, 시골

3 famous

famous

유명한

4 health

health

건강

5 label

label

표, 상표

6   **cute**

cute

귀여운

7   **sunflower**

sunflower

해바라기

8   **present**

present

선물

9   **theater**

theater

극장

10   **blame**

blame

비난하다

Unit Review

배운 내용 스스로 정리해보기

❶ 단수대명사 표

		주격	소유격	목적격	소유대명사
단수	1인칭	I	①	me	②
	2인칭	you	③	you	yours
	3인칭	④	his	him	his
		she	her	her	⑤
		it	⑥	it	-

❷ 주격

주격 인칭대명사는 _____ (으)로 해석한다.

예시문장 써보기

2인칭 단수 주격 사용하기

➜ _____

❸ 소유격

소유격 인칭대명사는 _____ (으)로 해석한다.

❹ 목적격

목적격 인칭대명사는 _____ (으)로 해석한다.

❺ 소유대명사

소유대명사는 ❶ _____ (으)로 ❷ _____ (으)로 해석한다.

UNIT 02

복수 대명사의 격

복수 주격	you, we, they
복수 소유격	your, our, their
복수 목적격	you, us, them

hobby	취미	team	팀
formula	공식	different	다른
bullet	총알	seek	찾다
idea	아이디어	enjoy	즐기다
dream	꿈	ceremony	의식, 식

UNIT **2** 복수 대명사의 격

❶ 복수대명사 표

복수 대명사의 표는 다음과 같다.

		주격	소유격	목적격	소유대명사
복수	1인칭	we	our	us	ours
	2인칭	you	your	you	yours
	3인칭	they	their	them	theirs

❷ 주격

주격 인칭대명사는 '~은/는/이/가'로 해석한다.

> We have the same hobby.
> Do you know this formula?
> They are good partners.

❸ 소유격

소유격 인칭대명사는 '~의'로 해석한다.

> It is our cat.
> Here are your presents.
> Brown is their favorite color.

❹ 목적격

목적격 인칭대명사는 '~을/를, ~에게'로 해석한다.

> Lora invited us for dinner.
> Gary wants to see you.
> Amy knows them very well.

❺ 소유대명사

소유대명사는 '소유격 + 명사'로 '~의 것'으로 해석한다.

> The hats are ours.
>
> The land is theirs.
>
> There are a lot of clothes. What is yours?

Activity 1

다음 인칭 대명사를 알맞은 주격 대명사에 연결해보세요.

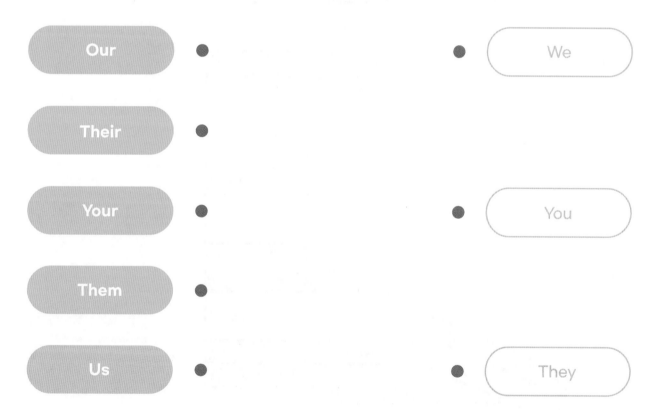

Activity 2

다음 중 줄마다 어색한 하나를 골라 색칠하세요.

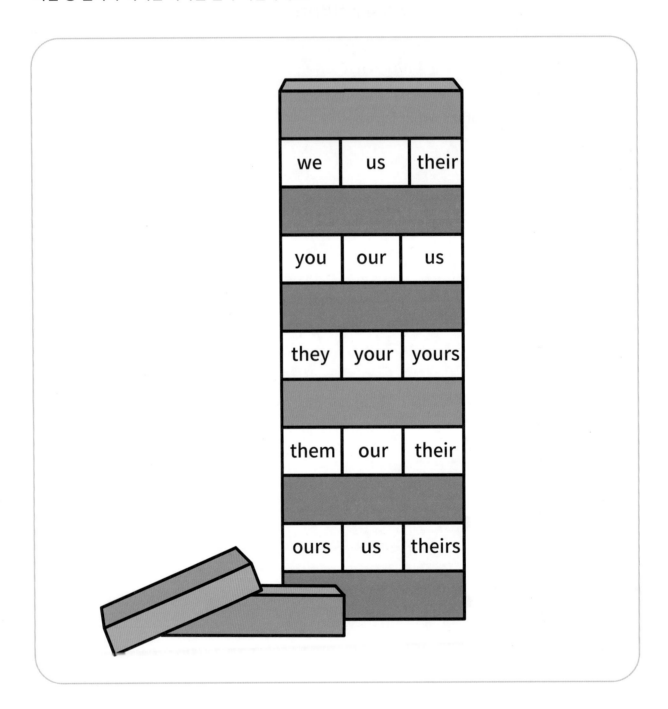

we	us	their
you	our	us
they	your	yours
them	our	their
ours	us	theirs

Exercise 1

알맞은 단어를 골라 문장을 완성하세요.

❶ **We / Our** team goes to the final.

❷ It is different from **ours / our** .

❸ He created **they / them** in the past.

❹ **They / Us** are looking for the lost bullets.

❺ The boxes are **yours / your** .

Exercise 2

빈칸에 알맞은 단어를 쓰세요.

❶ They are _____ students.
그들은 우리의 학생들이다.

❷ _____ should be quiet in the library.
너희들은 도서관에서 정숙해야 한다.

❸ I had a good time with _____ .
나는 그들과 좋은 시간을 보냈다.

❹ The house is _____ .
그 집은 우리의 것이다.

❺ _____ idea will be helpful.
너희들의 아이디어는 도움이 될 것이다.

1. A: Just write down ⬚⬚⬚⬚⬚ dream.

   B: Teacher, I want to be a doctor.

   (A) us

   (B) you

   (C) your

   (D) yours

2. A: ⬚⬚⬚⬚⬚ enjoy riding a bike.

   B: I want to join them.

   (A) They

   (B) Their

   (C) Them

   (D) Theirs

3. A: ⬚⬚⬚⬚⬚ meal is coming.

   B: I'm so hungry.

   (A) Us

   (B) We

   (C) Our

   (D) Ours

4. A: I'll secure ⬚⬚⬚⬚⬚ .

   B: Thank you so much.

   (A) we

   (B) our

   (C) your

   (D) yours

5. A: What are they doing?

   B: They start to hold ⬚⬚⬚⬚⬚

      ceremony.

   (A) they

   (B) their

   (C) them

   (D) thiers

⑥ A: Jane invited _____ to her birthday party.

　B: Let's go together.

　(A) we
　(B) us
　(C) our
　(D) ours

⑨ A: These presents are _____ .

　B: Oh, thank you so much.

　(A) you
　(B) our
　(C) your
　(D) yours

⑦ A: Can _____ solve this problem?
　B: I'm not sure.

　(A) we
　(B) our
　(C) their
　(D) theirs

⑩ A: Do _____ have to do it right away?

　B: No, we have some time.

　(A) us
　(B) we
　(C) our
　(D) your

⑧ A: It was a great meal.

　B: Popular restaurants have _____ own secret recipe.

　(A) us
　(B) our
　(C) they
　(D) their

1 hobby

취미

2 formula

공식

3 bullet

총알

4 idea

아이디어

5 dream

꿈

6 team
팀

7 different
다른

8 seek
찾다

9 enjoy
즐기다

10 ceremony
의식, 식

Unit Review

배운 내용 스스로 정리해보기

❶ 복수대명사 표

		주격	소유격	목적격	소유대명사
복수	1인칭	we	❶	❷	ours
	2인칭	❸	your	you	❹
	3인칭	they	their	❺	theirs

❷ 주격

주격 인칭대명사는 　　　　　 (으)로 해석한다.

예시문장 써보기

1인칭 복수 주격 사용하기

➜ _____

❸ 소유격

소유격 인칭대명사는 　　　　 (으)로 해석한다.

❹ 목적격

목적격 인칭대명사는 　　　　 (으)로 해석한다.

예시문장 써보기

1인칭 복수 목적격 사용하기

➜ _____

❺ 소유대명사

소유대명사는 ❶ 　　　　 (으)로 ❷ 　　　　 (으)로 해석한다.

UNIT 03

1, 2인칭 대명사의 활용

인칭대명사

1인칭	자기 자신 혹은 자기 자신이 포함된 집단을 칭하는 경우
2인칭	자기 자신이 아닌 상대방을 칭하는 경우

sign	서명하다, 조인하다	surprise	놀라게 하다
history	역사	campsite	캠프장
social	사회의	secret	비밀
use	사용하다, 쓰다	comment	논평, 언급
similar	비슷한	stress	스트레스

UNIT 3 1, 2인칭 대명사의 활용

1, 2인칭 대명사의 활용

		주격	소유격	목적격	소유대명사
1인칭	단수	I	my	me	mine
	복수	we	our	us	ours
2인칭	단수	you	your	you	yours
	복수	you	your	you	yours

1

Q Are you happy?
2인칭 단수 주격

A Yes, I am happy.
1인칭 단수 주격

2

Q What is your secret?
2인칭 단수 소유격

A My secret is this.
1인칭 단수 소유격

3

Q Where are you going?
2인칭 복수 주격

A We are going to a social club.
1인칭 복수 주격

4

Q Who is your history teacher?
2인칭 복수 소유격

A Our history teacher is Michael.
1인칭 복수 소유격

5

Q Do you love me?
2인칭 단수 주격   1인칭 단수 목적격

A Yes, I love you.
1인칭 단수 주격   2인칭 단수 목적격

6

Q Is Jane waiting for us?
1인칭 복수 목적격

A Yes, she is waiting for you.
3인칭 단수 주격   2인칭 복수 목적격

Q What is mine?
1인칭 단수 소유대명사

A This present is yours.
2인칭 단수 소유대명사

7

Q This computer doesn't work. Could I use yours?
1인칭 단수 주격   2인칭 복수 소유대명사

A Yes, you can use ours.
2인칭 단수 주격   1인칭 복수 소유대명사

8

Q Where are you?
2인칭 복수 주격

A Alex and I are in the cafe. We like this place.
1인칭 복수 주격

9

Activity 1

빈칸에 알맞은 인칭 대명사를 넣어 대화문을 완성해보세요.

Question	Answer
Am I late?	No, are on time.
Who is English teacher?	Our English teacher is Mr. McKellen
Where do you live?	live in an old farmhouse.
Were you waiting for ?	Yes, I was waiting for two of you.
Is that book yours?	No, it is not .
Where is our bag?	is the large one.

Activity 2

사다리를 타고 내려가 주어진 주격 인칭대명사의 소유격 인칭대명사를 작성해보세요.

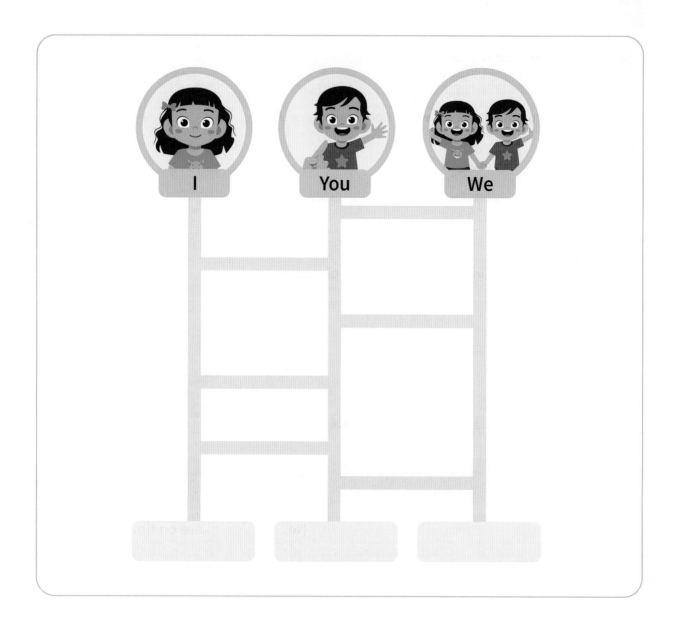

Exercise 1

알맞은 단어를 골라 문장을 완성하세요.

❶ Did **you / your** sign up for the class?

❷ **I / Me** got a high score in social studies.

❸ It will relieve **yours / your** stress.

❹ **We / our** are surprised to see him.

❺ Is this book **your / yours** ?

Exercise 2

빈칸에 알맞은 단어를 쓰세요.

❶ Where are _____ going?
우리는 어디로 가는 거니?

❷ Here is _____ campsite.
이곳이 너희들의 캠프장이다.

❸ Their costumes are similar to _____ .
그들의 복장은 우리의 것과 비슷하다.

❹ Can you help _____ ?
나를 도와줄 수 있어?

❺ I'll tell _____ some secrets.
너에게 몇몇 비밀을 말해줄게.

1 A: Can I use ▨▨▨▨▨ computer?

B: Of course.

(A) we

(B) you

(C) your

(D) yours

4 A: Describe your family.

B: Oh, It's hard for ▨▨▨▨▨ .

(A) I

(B) we

(C) our

(D) me

2 A: Thank you for your helpful comments.

B: It is ▨▨▨▨▨ duty.

(A) I

(B) me

(C) my

(D) mine

5 A: I found some money on the floor.

B: But, it's not ▨▨▨▨▨ .

(A) we

(B) our

(C) you

(D) yours

3 A: Did you go to the gym yesterday?

B: No, ▨▨▨▨▨ am still tired.

(A) I

(B) my

(C) we

(D) our

6 A: What is Julie doing?

B: She is cooking for _____ .

(A) us

(B) we

(C) our

(D) ours

9 A: I don't like Amy.

B: But, she likes _____ .

(A) me

(B) my

(C) you

(D) your

7 A: Why don't we go to the concert?

B: Can _____ reserve seats?

(A) our

(B) you

(C) your

(D) yours

10 A: What is _____ ?

B: The black one is yours.

(A) my

(B) mine

(C) your

(D) yours

8 A: Why don't we go to the theater?

B: But, _____ don't have much time.

(A) us

(B) we

(C) our

(D) your

1 **sign**
서명하다, 조인하다

2 **history**
역사

3 **social**
사회의

4 **use**
사용하다, 쓰다

5 **similar**
비슷한

6 **surprise**
놀라게 하다

surprise

7 **campsite**
캠프장

campsite

8 **secret**
비밀

secret

9 **comment**
논평, 언급

comment

10 **stress**
스트레스

stress

Unit Review

배운 내용 스스로 정리해보기

		주격	소유격	목적격	소유대명사
1인칭	단수	I	①	me	②
	복수	③	our	④	ours
2인칭	단수	you	your	⑤	⑥
	복수	you	⑦	you	yours

1, 2인칭 대명사의 활용

예시문장 써보기

① Are you joyful?에 대한 답변

→ _____

② Do you trust me?에 대한 답변

→ _____

③ What is your favorite color?에 대한 답변

→ _____

④ 1인칭 복수 소유격 사용하기

→ _____

⑤ 2인칭 복수 소유대명사 사용하기

→ _____

UNIT 04

3인칭 대명사의 활용

3인칭 단수	자기자신과 상대방이 아닌 제3자 한 명을 칭하는 경우
3인칭 복수	자기자신과 상대방이 아닌 제3자 여러 명을 칭하는 경우

laundry	세탁물	magazine	잡지
sore	아픈	bark	짖다
essay	과제물	lecture	강의
jaw	턱	earn	얻다
paw	발	escape	도망가다

3인칭 대명사의 활용

		주격	소유격	목적격	소유대명사
3인칭	단수	he	his	him	his
		she	her	her	hers
		it	its	it	-
	복수	they	their	them	theirs

1

Q Who is Craig?

A He is my brother.
3인칭 단수 주격 1인칭 단수 소유격

2

Q Who is the woman next to Dann?

A She is his girlfriend.
3인칭 단수 주격 3인칭 단수 소유격

3

Q Who do you want to meet?
2인칭 단수 주격

A I want to meet him. I like his essays.
3인칭 단수 목적격 3인칭 단수 소유격

4

Q What is Genie doing?

A She is doing her laundry.
3인칭 단수 주격 3인칭 단수 소유격

5

Q When is Gwen's birthday?

A Her birthday is tomorrow.
3인칭 단수 소유격

6

Q Who bought these things?

A Vella bought them. Everything is hers.
3인칭 단수 목적격 3인칭 단수 소유대명사

7

Q What is your cat doing?
2인칭 단수 소유격

A It is licking its paws.
3인칭 단수 주격   3인칭 단수 소유격

8

Q What is your favorite magazine?
2인칭 단수 소유격

A My favorite magazine is this one. / I love it too.
1인칭 단수 소유격   1인칭 단수 주격   3인칭 단수 목적격

9

Q Where are Jane and Sally?

A They are spending their time with some friends in the library.
3인칭 복수 주격   3인칭 복수 소유격

10

Q Whose pictures are these?

A These are theirs.
3인칭 복수 소유대명사

Activity 1

빈칸에 알맞은 인칭 대명사를 넣어 대화문을 완성해보세요.

Question	Answer
Is your father at home?	No, isn't.
How are your parents?	are very well.
How is your brother?	He doesn't like job.
Is this book or hers?	It's his.
What do you think about their uniform?	Ours is much nicer than .

Activity 2

인칭대명사를 활용하여 빈칸을 채우세요.

❶ She likes ⬚⬚⬚⬚ doll.
❷ The doll is ⬚⬚⬚⬚ .

❶ He loves ⬚⬚⬚⬚ .
❷ She loves ⬚⬚⬚⬚ .

❶ ⬚⬚⬚⬚ is my wallet.
❷ ⬚⬚⬚⬚ color is red.

Exercise 1

알맞은 단어를 골라 문장을 완성하세요.

❶ **He / Him** had a sore throat.

❷ I'm waiting for **they / them** .

❸ **It / Its** jaw is so strong.

❹ These magazines are **hers / her** .

❺ She believes **his / him** .

Exercise 2

빈칸에 알맞은 단어를 쓰세요.

❶ _____ car went into a slide.
그의 차가 미끄러졌다.

❷ She escaped from _____ .
그녀는 그들로부터 빠져 나왔다.

❸ The dog is _____ .
그 강아지는 그녀의 것이다.

❹ Can _____ play the violin?
그는 바이올린을 켤 수 있는가?

❺ _____ will start soon.
이것은 곧 시작할 것이다.

✏ Sentence Completion ━━━━━━━━━━━━━━━━━━━━━━

1 A: How much does it cost?

　B: ▨▨▨▨▨ costs 5 dollars.

(A) It

(B) Its

(C) They

(D) Them

2 A: How was her lecture?

　B: She made ▨▨▨▨▨ very easy and fun.

(A) it

(B) its

(C) them

(D) theirs

3 A: My dog seems nervous.

　B: Yeah, ▨▨▨▨▨ barks to me.

(A) it

(B) its

(C) they

(D) them

4 A: He earned a lot of money.

　B: But, ▨▨▨▨▨ work is so hard.

(A) it

(B) he

(C) his

(D) him

5 A: Where are the cacti?

　B: ▨▨▨▨▨ are located in the desert.

(A) They

(B) Their

(C) Them

(D) Theirs

6 A: She wears a new skirt.

B: I want to have a similar one with

_____.

(A) its

(B) she

(C) her

(D) hers

9 A: Kelly and her friend will go to the park.

B: I don't want to join _____.

(A) me

(B) her

(C) you

(D) them

7 A: Wow, look at that tower.

B: _____ height is amazing.

(A) It

(B) Its

(C) They

(D) Them

10 A: We should take a train to go there.

B: _____ is too far from here.

(A) It

(B) Its

(C) They

(D) Theirs

8 A: He and she are on the roof.

B: Why are _____ there.

(A) he

(B) we

(C) she

(D) they

1 **laundry**
세탁물

2 **sore**
아픈

3 **essay**
과제물

4 **jaw**
턱

5 **paw**
발

6 magazine
잡지

magazine

7 bark
짖다

bark

8 lecture
강의

lecture

9 earn
얻다

earn

10 escape
도망가다

escape

Unit Review

배운 내용 스스로 정리해보기

3인칭 대명사의 활용

		주격	소유격	목적격	소유대명사
3인칭	단수	he	❶	❷	his
		she	her	her	❸
		it	its	❹	-
	복수	❺	their	❻	theirs

예시문장 써보기

❶ What is Gina eating?에 대한 답변

→ _____

❷ When is Laura's birthday?에 대한 답변

→ _____

❸ Where is your cat?에 대한 답변

→ _____

❹ Where are Tony and Cindy?에 대한 답변

→ _____

❺ Who is the man on the bench?에 대한 답변

→ _____

TOSEL 실전문제 ②

PART A. Sentence Completion

DIRECTIONS: For questions 1 to 20, fill in the blanks to complete the sentences. Choose the option that BEST completes each blank.

지시 사항: 1번부터 20번까지는 빈칸을 알맞게 채워 대화를 완성하는 문제입니다. 가장 알맞은 답을 고르세요.

1. A: When is Gary's birthday?
   B: _____ birthday is tomorrow.

   (A) It

   (B) He

   (C) His

   (D) Him

2. A: Who is your English teacher?
   B: _____ English teacher is Jane

   (A) Us

   (B) We

   (C) You

   (D) Our

3. A: Which one is my book?
   B: That red one is _____.

   (A) you

   (B) your

   (C) yous

   (D) yours

4. A: Amy invited _____ to the party.
   B: Let's go together.

   (A) we

   (B) us

   (C) our

   (D) your

5. A: Which one is mine?
   B: The black one is _____.

   (A) you

   (B) your

   (C) yours

   (D) yoursen

6. A: She admires her father.
   B: What is _____ job?

   (A) he
   (B) his
   (C) she
   (D) her

7. A: Is this Mr. and Mrs. Jo's house?
   B: Yes, it is _____.

   (A) they
   (B) their
   (C) them
   (D) theirs

8. A: My sister graduated last week!
   B: Wow, congratulations to _____.

   (A) him
   (B) her
   (C) ours
   (D) their

9. A: Is that your hat?
   B: No, it's not _____. Maybe it's Mina's.

   (A) me
   (B) my
   (C) mine
   (D) the mine

10. A: When is _____ birthday?
    B: My birthday is in June.

    (A) my
    (B) her
    (C) your
    (D) their

11. A: What are _____ doing?
    B: They are preparing for the school festival.

    (A) we

    (B) he

    (C) she

    (D) they

12. A: I like that girl group.
    B: _____ song is also cheerful to me.

    (A) She

    (B) Her

    (C) They

    (D) Their

13. A: There are many people in the park.
    B: _____ are waiting for the concert.

    (A) We

    (B) You

    (C) They

    (D) Them

14. A: What are these things?
    B: Lucy bought _____ yesterday.

    (A) us

    (B) her

    (C) them

    (D) theirs

15. A: What is your hobby?
    B: _____ hobby is playing computer games.

    (A) I

    (B) My

    (C) His

    (D) Your

16. A: His novel is so famous.
    B: I also like _____.

    (A) its
    (B) me
    (C) his
    (D) you

17. A: What is your favorite movie?
    B: _____ favorite movie is Harry Potter.

    (A) I
    (B) My
    (C) You
    (D) Your

18. A: These cookies are _____.
    B: Wow, these look delicious.

    (A) our
    (B) you
    (C) your
    (D) yours

19. A: He often blames himself.
    B: We should cheer _____ up.

    (A) he
    (B) his
    (C) him
    (D) hime

20. A: I like my new cup.
    B: I'm glad _____ like it.

    (A) I
    (B) me
    (C) you
    (D) your

CHAPTER 03

III. 동사

UNIT 01

동사의 기본시제

기본시제

현재	지금 있는 일을 나타냄
과거	예전에 있었던 일을 나타냄
미래	앞으로 일어날 일을 나타냄

진행시제

현재	지금 일어나고 있는 일을 나타냄
과거	예전에 일어나고 있었던 일을 나타냄
미래	앞으로 일어나고 있을 일을 나타냄

agree	동의하다	assignment	과제
audience	관중	holiday	휴일
stay	계속 있다	declare	선언하다
stop	멈추다	apply	신청하다
agreement	동의	fail	실패하다

UNIT ① 동사의 기본 시제

❶ 현재시제

주어	be 동사	have 동사	일반동사
1인칭 단수 **I**	am	have	동사원형
1인칭 복수 **We**	are		
2인칭 단수, 복수 **You**	are		
3인칭 단수 **He, She, It**	is	has	'동사원형+-(e)s'
3인칭 복수 **They**	are	have	동사원형

I am a student. 현재의 상태

He is ten years old. 현재의 상태

I have three daughters. 현재의 상태

She has blue eyes. 현재의 상태

We go to school every day. 현재의 습관적·반복적 행위

He visits there tomorrow. 미래시제 대용

❷ 과거시제

주어	be 동사	have 동사	일반동사
1인칭 단수 **I**	was	had	'동사원형+-(e)d'
1인칭 복수 **We**	were		
2인칭 단수, 복수 **You**	were		
3인칭 단수 **He, She, It**	was		
3인칭 복수 **They**	were		

I was at the campsite. 과거의 상태

They were happy. 과거의 상태

He had a lot of money. 과거의 상태

She usually played a board game in those days. 과거의 습관적·반복적 행위

❸ 미래시제

'will+동사원형', 'be going to+동사원형' 등을 사용한다.

I will stay with them tomorrow. 미래의 예정

I am going to apply for the lecture tomorrow. 미래의 예정

❹ 진행형

주어	현재진행	과거진행	미래진행
1인칭 단수 I	'am + -ing'	'was + -ing'	
1인칭 복수 We	'are + -ing'	'were + -ing'	
2인칭 단수, 복수 You	'are + -ing'	'were + -ing'	'will be + -ing'
3인칭 단수 He, She, It	'is + -ing'	'was + -ing'	
3인칭 복수 They	'are + -ing'	'were + -ing'	

She is singing a song in front of many audiences. 현재 진행 중인 동작

They were watching a movie in their house. 과거 어느 시점의 진행 중인 동작

I will be playing the piano here tomorrow. 미래 한 시점에서의 동작의 진행

Activity 1

다음 주어를 알맞은 동사에 연결해보세요. (복수 정답 가능)

I ●   ● are

You ●   ● has

He ●   ● am

We ●   ● were

Activity 2

알맞은 단어와 모두 연결해보세요.

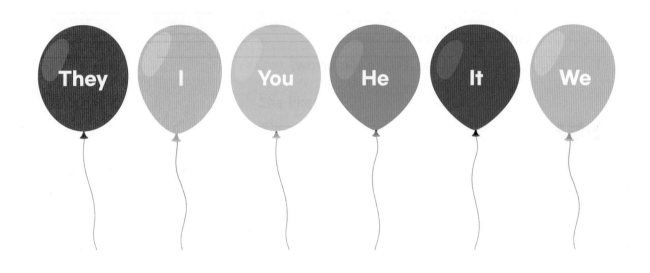

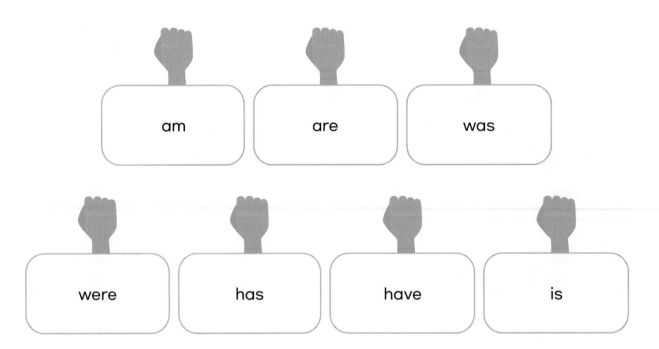

Exercise 1

알맞은 단어를 골라 문장을 완성하세요.

❶ **I / He** agree with you.

❷ She **are / is** a good student.

❸ He **loves / love** his mother.

❹ **We / I** are going to the park.

❺ They **declares / declare** a peace agreement.

Exercise 2

보기의 단어를 적절한 형태로 활용하여, 빈칸에 알맞은 단어를 쓰세요.

보기	finish	is	drive	like	stop

❶ They _____ fighting each other.
그들은 서로 싸우는 것을 멈춘다.

❷ She _____ staying at home.
그녀는 집에서 머무르는 중이다.

❸ I _____ to study English.
나는 영어 공부하는 것을 좋아한다.

❹ He _____ a truck.
그는 트럭을 운전한다.

❺ She _____ her assignment.
그녀는 그녀의 과제를 끝낸다.

Sentence Completion

1 A: What will you eat for lunch?

 B: I will　　　　　　a hamburger.

(A) order

(B) orders

(C) orderes

(D) ordering

4 A: They will　　　　　　a lot of
 people.

 B: Oh, I will apply for it.

(A) hire

(B) hired

(C) hires

(D) hiring

2 A: How was your holiday?

 B: We　　　　　　a good time.

(A) has

(B) had

(C) have

(D) having

5 A: I　　　　　　to pass the exam.

 B: Cheer up.

(A) fails

(B) failes

(C) failed

(D) failing

3 A: Where is he?

 B: He is　　　　　　in Seoul now.

(A) live

(B) lives

(C) lived

(D) living

6 A: My mother _____ me to play with friends.

B: That sounds great.

(A) allow

(B) allows

(C) allowd

(D) allowing

9 A: I'll _____ the fancy shoes someday.

B: What brand do you like?

(A) buy

(B) buys

(C) buying

(D) bought

7 A: Oh, the dog is _____ me.

B: Maybe he likes you.

(A) bite

(B) bites

(C) bited

(D) biting

10 A: I _____ "Lola's Adventure" yesterday.

B: That's quite an interesting action movie.

(A) watch

(B) watched

(C) watches

(D) watching

8 A: What are you doing?

B: I'm _____ for olive oil.

(A) look

(B) looks

(C) looking

(D) looked

1 **agree**

동의하다

2 **audience**

관중

3 **stay**

계속 있다

4 **stop**

멈추다

5 **agreement**

동의

6 **assignment** assignment

과제

7 **holiday** holiday

휴일

8 **declare** declare

선언하다

9 **apply** apply

신청하다

10 **fail** fail

실패하다

Unit Review

배운 내용 스스로 정리해보기

❶ 현재시제

예시문장 써보기

She가 주어인 have동사의 현재시제

➜ _____

❷ 과거시제

예시문장 써보기

We가 주어인 be동사의 과거시제

➜ _____

❸ 미래시제

예시문장 써보기

They가 주어일 때 be going to 사용하기

➜ _____

❹ 진행형

예시문장 써보기

I가 주어인 과거진행형

➜ _____

UNIT 02

동사의 불규칙 과거형

규칙 과거형	동사원형 + -(e)d
불규칙 과거형	정해진 규칙이 없으며, 현재형과 동일한 경우도 있음

begin	시작하다	meet	만나다
catch	잡다	cut	자르다
hit	때리다	fall	떨어지다
bring	가져오다	keep	유지하다
lose	잃어버리다	let	허락하다

UNIT ② 동사의 불규칙 과거형

❶ 불규칙 과거형 표

현재형	불규칙 과거형	현재형	불규칙 과거형
go	went	say	said
come	came	keep	kept
become	became	hear	heard
sit	sat	think	thought
drink	drank	know	knew
eat	ate	fall	fell
find	found	give	gave
see	saw	buy	bought
buy	bought	take	took
meet	met	send	sent
run	ran	sleep	slept
bring	brought	make	made
tell	told	leave	left

I went downstairs two hours ago.

My grandmother told me a fairy tale the day before yesterday.

He heard my story last weekend.

The boy slept at nine yesterday.

I bought a new car last month.

She thought for a moment before saying.

I found the key on the table.

We met at the station.

I saw a beautiful flower on the way home.

She gave a cup of water to me.

❷ 현재형과 과거형이 같은 경우

현재형	불규칙 과거형	현재형	불규칙 과거형
put	put	cut	cut
hit	hit	cost	cost
hurt	hurt	let	let

I put the book on the desk yesterday.

He cut the grass last week.

Amy hit the ball too hard last time.

She bought a new dress. It cost about 100 dollars.

My parents let me drive a car last year.

Activity 1

다음 동사의 알맞은 과거형에 연결해보세요.

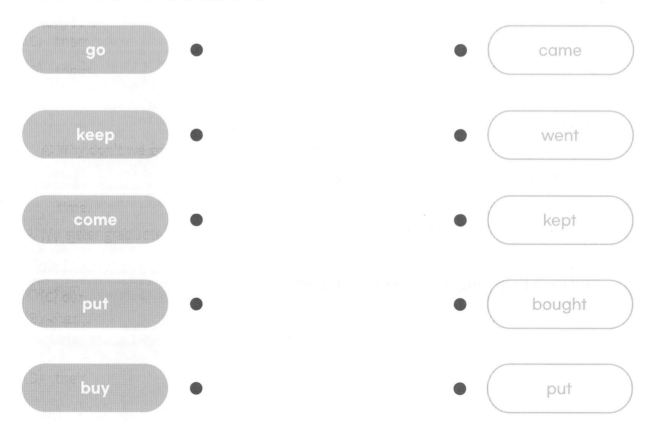

go		came
keep		went
come		kept
put		bought
buy		put

Activity 2

다음 퍼즐에서 현재형과 과거형이 같은 단어를 모두 찾고 그 단어를 활용하여 문장을 완성하세요.

C	U	T	K	A	L	D
O	H	P	B	R	E	F
S	U	Z	C	P	L	Q
L	M	X	H	U	R	T
B	E	V	E	T	O	C
A	R	T	C	H	I	T
C	H	C	O	S	T	A

❶ I _____ the paper into two pieces.

❷ _____ the puppy come into the room.

❸ Don't _____ your cup on my table.

❹ This bag _____ more than that one.

❺ The bat _____ the ball and made a loud noise.

❻ I went to the hospital because my thumb _____ .

Exercise 1

올바른 형태의 과거형을 골라 문장을 완성하세요.

❶ He **cut / cutted** a piece of paper.

❷ She **eated / ate** a dessert.

❸ The woman **bought / brought** a bracelet at the shop.

❹ Teacher **gived / gave** me a book.

❺ I **heared / heard** his voice.

Exercise 2

보기의 단어를 적절한 형태로 활용하여, 주어진 문장을 완성하세요.

보기   lose   leave   catch   put   begin

❶ They _____ some birds.
그들은 새 몇 마리를 잡았다.

❷ The meeting _____ at ten in the morning.
회의는 아침 10시에 시작했다.

❸ He _____ his wallet.
그는 그의 지갑을 잃어버렸다.

❹ She _____ early.
그녀는 일찍 떠났다.

❺ Someone _____ a box here yesterday.
어제 누군가가 박스를 여기에 두었다.

Sentence Completion

1. A: I _____ what he did.
   B: Tell me about it.

   (A) am
   (B) was
   (C) knew
   (D) knowed

2. A: He _____ an email to you.
   B: I will check it soon.

   (A) send
   (B) sent
   (C) senti
   (D) sended

3. A: I _____ him on the bench.
   B: Why was he there?

   (A) find
   (B) found
   (C) finded
   (D) founded

4. A: How is she?
   B: She _____ to a hospital.

   (A) go
   (B) god
   (C) goed
   (D) went

5. A: Do you know him?
   B: I _____ him yesterday.

   (A) met
   (B) meet
   (C) meeted
   (D) meeten

6 A: Where did you find your wallet?

B: Losa found and _____ it to me.

(A) give

(B) gave

(C) given

(D) gived

9 A: Did you fix the car?

B: Yes, it _____ a lot of money.

(A) cos

(B) cost

(C) costed

(D) costing

7 A: I _____ a dragon in my dream.

B: Was it a big dragon?

(A) see

(B) our

(C) saw

(D) sawn

10 A: What happened to his face?

B: Owen _____ him in the face.

(A) hit

(B) hitted

(C) hitten

(D) was hit

8 A: She already _____ the hospital.

B: I'll call her right away.

(A) left

(B) leave

(C) leavf

(D) leaved

UNIT 2 동사의 불규칙 과거형

1 begin
시작하다

begin

2 catch
잡다

catch

3 hit
때리다

hit

4 bring
가져오다

bring

5 lose
잃어버리다

lose

6 **meet**
만나다

meet

7 **cut**
자르다

cut

8 **fall**
넘어지다

fall

9 **keep**
유지하다

keep

10 **let**
허락하다

let

Unit Review

배운 내용 스스로 정리해보기

❶ **불규칙 과거형**

예시문장 써보기

① become의 과거형 사용하기

➜ _____

② come의 과거형 사용하기

➜ _____

③ take의 과거형 사용하기

➜ _____

④ meet의 과거형 사용하기

➜ _____

❷ **현재형과 과거형이 같은 경우**

예시문장 써보기

① put의 과거형 사용하기

➜ _____

② cut의 과거형 사용하기

➜ _____

③ cost의 과거형 사용하기

➜ _____

④ hurt의 과거형 사용하기

➜ _____

UNIT 03

헷갈리기 쉬운 동사

주어	현재 긍정형 & 부정형		과거 긍정형 & 부정형	
I **We** **You** **They**	do	do not (don't)	did	did not (didn't)
He **She** **It**	does	does not (doesn't)		

stubborn	고집에 센	**clue**	단서
mistake	실수	**laptop**	노트북
early	이른	**enough**	충분한
honest	정직한	**fight**	싸우다
ago	~ 전에	**busy**	바쁜

UNIT ③ 헷갈리기 쉬운 동사

❶ be동사의 부정형과 과거형

주어		부정형	부정형(축약형)	과거형	과거 부정형
1인칭 단수	I	am not	I'm not	was	was not (wasn't)
1인칭 복수	We	are not	We're not / We aren't	were	were not (weren't)
2인칭 단수, 복수	You	are not	You're not / You aren't	were	were not (weren't)
3인칭 단수	He, She, It	is not	He's not / He isn't	was	was not (wasn't)
3인칭 복수	They	are not	They're not / They aren't	were	were not (weren't)

I am not a doctor.

You are not slow.

She is not stubborn.

I was on the bed an hour ago.

We were sick last night.

It was my mistake.

❷ do(does)의 부정형과 과거형

주어		부정형	부정형(축약형)	과거형	과거 부정형
1인칭 단수	I	do not	don't	did	did not (didn't)
1인칭 복수	We	do not	don't	did	did not (didn't)
2인칭 단수, 복수	You	do not	don't	did	did not (didn't)
3인칭 단수	He, She, It	does not	doesn't	did	did not (didn't)
3인칭 복수	They	do not	don't	did	did not (didn't)

I do not eat a kiwi.

She does not drink a cup of coffee.

They do not go home early.

He did a great job yesterday.

❸ have(has)의 부정형과 과거형

주어		부정형	부정형(축약형)	과거형	과거 부정형
1인칭 단수	I				
1인칭 복수	We	do not have	don't have		
2인칭 단수, 복수	You			had	did not have (didn't have)
3인칭 단수	He, She, It	does not have	doesn't have		
3인칭 복수	They	do not have	don't have		

I do not have an umbrella.

She does not have a clue.

They do not have enough time.

He didn't have a laptop computer.

Activity 1

다음 동사의 알맞은 부정형, 과거형 동사에 연결해보세요.

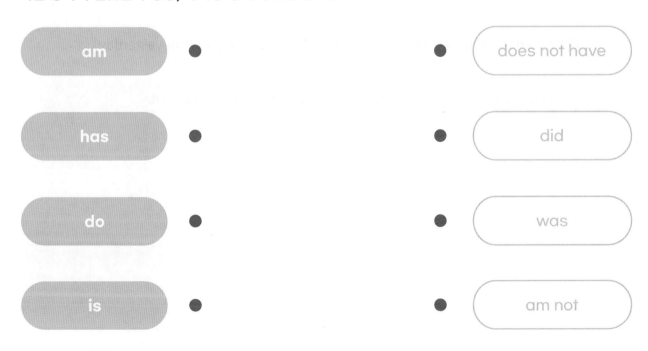

am •   • does not have

has •   • did

do •   • was

is •   • am not

Activity 2

올바른 부정형/과거형 문장의 번호를 쓰세요.

❶ We were sick last night.

❷ She do not have an umbrella.

❸ They do not go home early.

❹ He did a great job yesterday.

❺ It were my mistake.

❻ I does not eat a kiwi.

Exercise 1

알맞은 단어를 골라 문장을 완성하세요.

❶ He   **is not / am not**   a doctor.

❷ She   **was / were**   an honest student.

❸ They   **doesn't / don't**   have computers.

❹ It   **are not / is not**   my decision.

❺ She   **wasn't / didn't**   drink milk yesterday.

Exercise 2

빈칸에 알맞은 단어를 쓰세요.

❶ He _____ not shy.
그는 수줍어하지 않는다.

❷ I don't _____ enough money.
나는 충분한 돈을 가지고 있지 않다.

❸ It _____ hard for me.
그것은 나에게 어려운 일이었다.

❹ They didn't _____ to the zoo last week.
그들은 지난 주에 동물원에 가지 않았다.

❺ Where _____ you at 11 o'clock last Friday morning?
지난주 금요일 아침 11시에 너는 어디에 있었니?

Sentence Completion

1 A: Where is she?

   B: She _____ work this week.

(A) don't
(B) didn't
(C) wasn't
(D) doesn't

4 A: He is watching TV.

   B: Maybe he _____ not busy now.

(A) is
(B) am
(C) are
(D) was

2 A: He _____ not in school.
   B: Then, where was he?

(A) am
(B) are
(C) was
(D) were

5 A: We _____ have enough time.
   B: Hurry up.

(A) don't
(B) is not
(C) are not
(D) doesn't

3 A: We need some paper for art class.

   B: I _____ have enough.

(A) don't
(B) are not
(C) am not
(D) doesn't

6 A: They   talk to me.

B: Did you fight with them?

(A) don't

(B) doesn't

(C) are not

(D) am not

9 A: He doesn't   one
similar to yours.

B: I'll check it later.

(A) has

(B) had

(C) have

(D) having

7 A: You were the second place in the contest!

B: But it   not a gold medal.

(A) is

(B) do

(C) am

(D) are

10 A: We   not in the
classroom at that time.

B: Then, who opened the door?

(A) are

(B) was

(C) had

(D) were

8 A: I don't   his bad table
manners.

B: I think so too.

(A) like

(B) likes

(C) liked

(D) liking

1 **stubborn**

고집이 센

2 **mistake**

실수

3 **early**

이른

4 **honest**

정직한

5 **ago**

~전에

6 **clue**
단서

clue

7 **laptop**
노트북

laptop

8 **enough**
충분한

enough

9 **fight**
싸우다

fight

10 **busy**
바쁜

busy

Unit Review

배운 내용 스스로 정리해보기

❶ be동사의 부정형과 과거형

예시문장 써보기

① 주어가 He인 현재시제 be동사의 부정형 사용하기

➜ _____

② 주어가 We인 be동사의 과거형 사용하기

➜ _____

❷ do(does)의 부정형과 과거형

예시문장 써보기

① 주어가 It일 때의 부정형

➜ _____

② 주어가 I일 때의 과거형

➜ _____

❸ have(has)의 부정형과 과거형

예시문장 써보기

① 주어가 She일 때의 부정형

➜ _____

② 주어가 They일 때의 과거형

➜ _____

UNIT 04

조동사

	과거형	의미
will	would	~할 것이다
can	could	~할 수 있다
may	might	~해도 된다
must	had to	~해야만 한다

license	허가하다	cancel	취소하다
difference	차이	cheat	속이다
borrow	빌리다	understand	이해하다
passport	여권	ask	질문하다
find	찾다	believe	믿다

UNIT ④ 조동사

본동사와 함께 쓰여 본동사에 가능·허가·의무·추측 등의 의미를 더해주는 동사를 조동사라고 한다.

긍정문에서는 '**주어 + 조동사 + 동사원형**…'의 형태로 쓰이며,
부정문에서는 '**주어 + 조동사 + not + 동사원형**…'의 형태로 쓰인다.

❶ will · would

- will – will not [won't]
- would – would not [wouldn't] will의 과거형

① **의지 · 추측**

I will find a new way tomorrow.

He will not [won't] be there now.

② **제안 · 요청**

Will [Would] you lend me the map?

③ **습관 · 경향**

Dogs will wag their tails.

He would understand difficult formulas.

❷ can · could

- can – can not [can't]
- could – could not [couldn't] can의 과거형

① **능력 · 가능**

I can not [can't] believe in you.

② **부탁 · 허가**

Can [Could] I ask a question?

③ **추측**

He can not [can't] cancel the schedule.

❸ may · might

· may - may not [mayn't]
· might - might not [mightn't] may의 과거형

---

❶ 허가

May I see your driver's license?

❷ 불확실한 추측

Most things change. The difference may not [mayn't] be eternal.

❸ 기원

May you live long!

---

❹ must

· must (= have to) - must not [mustn't]
· had to must의 과거형

---

❶ 강한 의무

You had to go home early.

❷ 금지

You must not cheat me.

❸ 강한 추측

He must be honest.

Activity 1

다음 조동사의 알맞은 과거형 동사에 연결해보세요.

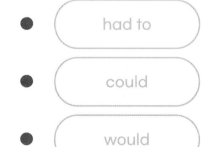

Activity 2

미로를 따라 각 조동사의 과거형을 빈칸에 쓰세요.

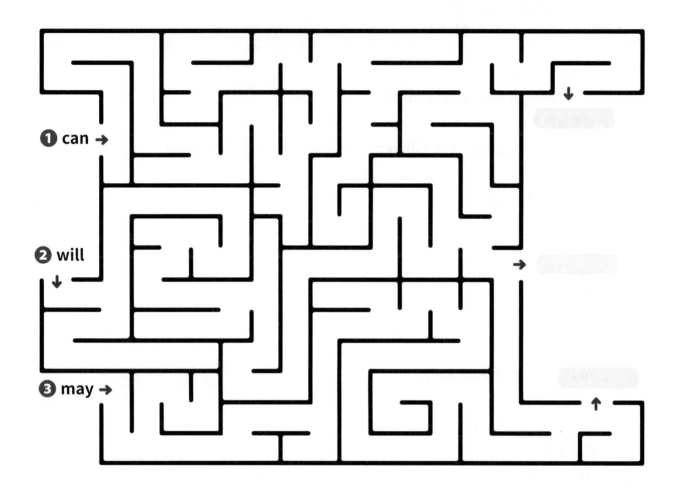

❶ can →

❷ will →

❸ may →

Exercise 1

알맞은 단어를 골라 문장을 완성하세요.

❶ He can **go / goes** to school early.

❷ **Can / Must** I ask a question?

❸ They **musted / had to** clean the room first.

❹ May I **borrow / borrowed** your pencil?

❺ She **not will / will not** come back home tonight.

Exercise 2

빈칸에 알맞은 단어를 쓰세요.

❶ You _____ not cheat someone.
너는 다른 사람을 속이면 안된다.

❷ He _____ solve the problem.
그는 그 문제를 해결할 수 있다.

❸ She _____ cancel the reservation.
그녀는 예약을 취소할 것이다.

❹ _____ I drink your water?
너의 물을 좀 마셔도 될까?

❺ We _____ take the stairs.
우리는 계단을 이용할 것이다.

Sentence Completion

1 A: Did you finish your homework?

B: I _____ do it after dinner.

(A) will

(B) could

(C) would

(D) will not

2 A: Aren't you tired?

B: I can _____ this all day.

(A) do

(B) did

(C) was

(D) does

3 A: We _____ reserve two seats.

B: Ok, I'll do it right away.

(A) will

(B) must

(C) could

(D) had to

4 A: _____ I check your passport?

B: Ok, here it is.

(A) Will

(B) May

(C) Must

(D) Would

5 A: Do you know what color his car is?

B: It _____ be a blue one.

(A) can

(B) will

(C) may

(D) could

6 A: The man _____ have gone out through another gate.

B: Ok, let's find it.

(A) will
(B) might
(C) will not
(D) might not

9 A: It _____ help ease the pain.

B: I hope it will be effective.

(A) had
(B) may
(C) can't
(D) had to

7 A: We must _____ the exam.

B: But, it's too hard.

(A) pass
(B) passes
(C) passed
(D) passing

10 A: You _____ wear swimming goggles in the pool.

B: Oh, I forgot to bring it.

(A) can
(B) may
(C) have
(D) must

8 A: We can _____ sharks in the aquarium.

B: I want to see them.

(A) see
(B) saw
(C) sees
(D) seeing

UNIT 4 조동사

1 **license**
허가하다

license

2 **difference**
차이

difference

3 **borrow**
빌리다

borrow

4 **passport**
여권

passport

5 **find**
찾다

find

6 **cancel**
취소하다

7 **cheat**
속이다

8 **understand**
이해하다

UNIT 4 조동사

9 **ask**
질문하다

10 **believe**
믿다

Unit Review

배운 내용 스스로 정리해보기

❶ will · would

조동사 will의 과거형은 ❶ [   ] 이고 부정형은 ❷ [   ], ❸ [   ] (이)다.

예시문장 써보기

긍정의 제안·요청

➜ _____

❷ can · could

조동사 can의 과거형은 ❶ [   ] 이고 부정형은 ❷ [   ], ❸ [   ] (이)다.

예시문장 써보기

부정의 추측

➜ _____

❸ may · might

조동사 may의 과거형은 ❶ [   ] 이고 부정형은 ❷ [   ], ❸ [   ] (이)다.

예시문장 써보기

긍정의 허가

➜ _____

❹ must

조동사 must는 ❶ [   ] (으)로 바꿔쓸 수 있고, 과거형이 따로 없기 때문에 과거형은

❷ [   ] 로 쓰며, 부정형은 ❸ [   ] (이)다.

예시문장 써보기

강한 의무의 과거형

➜ _____

TOSEL 실전문제 ❸

SECTION II. Reading and Writing

PART A. Sentence Completion

DIRECTIONS: For questions 1 to 20, fill in the blanks to complete the sentences. Choose the option that BEST completes each blank.

지시 사항: 1번부터 20번까지는 빈칸을 알맞게 채워 대화를 완성하는 문제입니다. 가장 알맞은 답을 고르세요.

1. A: Where were you?
    B: I _____ in the hospital.

    (A) am

    (B) are

    (C) was

    (D) were

2. A: You _____ go home early.
    B: Ok, I'll go back soon.

    (A) can

    (B) must

    (C) could

    (D) had to

3. A: Why don't we go to a cafe?
    B: But, I _____ have a laptop computer.

    (A) do not

    (B) am not

    (C) are not

    (D) does not

4. A: What did you eat for lunch?
    B: I _____ just a sandwich.

    (A) eat

    (B) ate

    (C) eaten

    (D) eated

5. A: He _____ go abroad tomorrow.
    B: Oh, I'll miss him.

    (A) will

    (B) can

    (C) must

    (D) would

6. A: She _____ the documents on the desk yesterday.
    B: But, I can't find it.

    (A) put

    (B) puts

    (C) puted

    (D) putted

7. A: What were you doing last night?
    B: We _____ watching TV in my house.

    (A) are

    (B) was

    (C) were

    (D) have

8. A: Can I ask some questions?
    B: But I _____ your teacher.

    (A) was

    (B) do not

    (C) am not

    (D) does not

9. A: He _____ a new car last week.
    B: I want to see it.

    (A) buy

    (B) buyed

    (C) bought

    (D) boughted

10. A: _____ I see your identification card?
    B: Yes, here it is.

    (A) Will

    (B) May

    (C) Must

    (D) Have to

11. A: How old is your brother?
    B: He _____ nine years old.

    (A) is

    (B) am

    (C) are

    (D) was

12. A: He _____ like to eat tomatoes.
    B: Ok, I'll pick them out.

    (A) do

    (B) does

    (C) is not

    (D) does not

13. A: It's too hot to run.
    B: I believe you _____ do it.

    (A) will

    (B) can

    (C) might

    (D) would

14. A: I _____ your card under the chair.
    B: Thank you so much.

    (A) finded

    (B) finden

    (C) found

    (D) founded

15. A: The deadline is tomorrow.
    B: I _____ have enough time to finish it.

    (A) am not

    (B) does not

    (C) was not

    (D) did not

16. A: How many erasers do you have?
    B: I _____ three.

    (A) is

    (B) are

    (C) has

    (D) have

17. A: Who's next?
    B: She _____ first.

    (A) came

    (B) come

    (C) comed

    (D) coming

18. A: Why _____ you late for school
       yesterday?
    B: I dropped by the hospital.

    (A) is

    (B) are

    (C) was

    (D) were

19. A: You _____ take your seat now.
    B: Thank you for your help.

    (A) may

    (B) might

    (C) had to

    (D) must to

20. A: Who spilled milk on the floor?
    B: I _____ clean it soon.

    (A) will go to

    (B) am going

    (C) will going

    (D) am going to

Answers

Short Answers

CHAPTER 1

UNIT 1 p.23

Activity
1. orange 2. violin 3. dinner / English 4. flower 5. English / dinner
(O) 1, 3, 4, 5, 7, 10, 12 (X) 2, 6, 8, 9, 11

Exercise 1 p.25
1. X 2. the 3. a 4. a 5. the

Exercise 2
1. the 2. A 3. the 4. the 5. X

Sentence Completion p.26
1. (B) 2. (A) 3. (A) 4. (B) 5. (A) 6. (C) 7. (D) 8. (A) 9. (B) 10. (A)

Unit Review p.30
1. ❶ 부정관사 ❶ ➡ There is a large box on the floor. ❷ ➡ I have an apple.
2. ❶ 정관사 ❶ ➡ I saw a cat. The cat was cute. ❷ ➡ I can play the guitar.
3. ❶ ➡ Let's play tennis. ❷ ➡ He likes mathematics.

UNIT 2 p.33

Activity
1. water 2. sugar 3. bread 4. paper 5. cake
1. a sheet of 2. a piece of 3. a slice of 4. a glass of
5. a piece of 6. a loaf of 7. a spoonful of 8. a bowl of

Exercise 1 p.35
1. English 2. Korea 3. glass 4. slice 5. loaves

Exercise 2
1. X 2. cup 3. spoon 4. glass 5. bottles

Sentence Completion p.36
1. (A) 2. (A) 3. (D) 4. (C) 5. (C) 6. (B) 7. (D) 8. (B) 9. (D) 10. (B)

Unit Review p.40
1. ❶ 고유명사 ❷ 추상명사 ❸ 물질명사
❶ ➡ I love Korea. ❷ ➡ She needs your advice.
2. ❶ a[갯수] + 단위명사 + of + 셀 수 없는 명사 ❶ ➡ My dad drinks a cup of coffee every day.
❷ ➡ I have a piece of paper. ❸ ➡ They baked two loaves of bread.

UNIT 3 p.43

Activity
1. cups, hands 2. companies, parties 3. tomatoes, churches, glasses, boxes 4. knives, wives
1. box, dish, knife

Exercise 1 p.45
1. cards 2. factories 3. seats 4. festivals 5. dishes

Exercise 2
1. Buses 2. animals 3. boys 4. wolves 5. tomatoes

Sentence Completion p.46
1. (C) 2. (B) 3. (D) 4. (B) 5. (B) 6. (D) 7. (D) 8. (A) 9. (C) 10. (B)

Unit Review p.50
1. ❷ 어미가 '모음 + y' ❸ 어미가 '모음 + o'
❶ ➡ I saw Bonita two days ago. ❷ ➡ Panda eat bamboos.
2. ❶ ➡ I have three watches. ❷ ➡ There are two ladies.
3. ❶ ➡ They have strong stomachs. ❷ ➡ Physics is interesting.

UNIT 4 p.53

Activity
1. sheep 2. men 3. teeth 4. media 5. oxen
1. deer → deer 2. sheep → sheep 3. salmon → salmon

Exercise 1 p.55
1. children 2. geese 3. mice 4. deer 5. women

Exercise 2
1. oxen 2. teeth 3. stimuli 4. salmon 5. people

Sentence Completion p.56
1. (A) 2. (A) 3. (B) 4. (A) 5. (A) 6. (A) 7. (B) 8. (C) 9. (A) 10. (B)

Unit Review p.60
1. ❶ ➡ Sheep are on the mountain. ❷ ➡ He saw many fish on the ship.
2. ❶ ➡ She has white teeth. ❷ ➡ Four men are on the sofa.
❸ ➡ There are many people in the bus. ❹ ➡ Children love candies.
❺ ➡ I don't understand the phenomena.

TOSEL 실전문제 1
1. (C) 2. (A) 3. (D) 4. (C) 5. (A) 6. (A) 7. (C) 8. (C) 9. (B) 10. (C)
11. (C) 12. (B) 13. (B) 14. (A) 15. (B) 16. (B) 17. (D) 18. (B) 19. (A) 20. (B)

| UNIT 1 p.69 | 1. mine | 2. Yours | 3. his | 4. her | 5. Its |
| Activity | 2. 단수대명사 표 참고 | | | | |

| Exercise 1 p.71 | 1. Your | 2. him | 3. mine | 4. it | 5. Her |

| Exercise 2 | 1. her | 2. him | 3. yours | 4. Its | 5. her |

| Sentence Completion p.72 | 1. (B) | 2. (B) | 3. (C) | 4. (D) | 5. (A) | 6. (C) | 7. (C) | 8. (C) | 9. (D) | 10. (C) |

Unit Review p.76	1. ① my	② mine	③ your		
	④ he	⑤ hers	⑥ its		
	2. ① ~은/는/이/가	① ➡ You know the truth.			
	3. ① 의	4. ① ~을/를, ~에게	5. ① 소유격 + 명사	② ~의 것	

| UNIT 2 p.79 | 1. We | 2. They | 3. You | 4. They | 5. We |
| Activity | 1. their | 2. you | 3. they | 4. our | 5. theirs |

| Exercise 1 p.81 | 1. Our | 2. ours | 3. them | 4. They | 5. yours |

| Exercise 2 | 1. our | 2. You | 3. them | 4. ours | 5. Your |

| Sentence Completion p.82 | 1. (C) | 2. (A) | 3. (C) | 4. (D) | 5. (B) | 6. (B) | 7. (A) | 8. (D) | 9. (D) | 10. (B) |

Unit Review p.86	1. ① our	② us	③ you	④ yours	⑤ them
	2. ① ~은/는/이/가		① ➡ We want to eat a spicy one.		
	3. ① 의	4. ① ~을/를, ~에게	① ➡ Tom invited us to the party.		
	5. ① 소유격 + 명사	② ~의 것			

UNIT 3 p.89	1. you	2. your	3. I / We		
Activity	4. us	5. mine	6. Ours		
	1. I - My	2. You - Your	3. We - Our		

| Exercise 1 p.91 | 1. you | 2. I | 3. your | 4. We | 5. yours |

| Exercise 2 | 1. we | 2. your | 3. ours | 4. me | 5. you |

| Sentence Completion p.92 | 1. (C) | 2. (C) | 3. (A) | 4. (D) | 5. (D) | 6. (A) | 7. (B) | 8. (B) | 9. (C) | 10. (B) |

Unit Review p.96	1. ① my	② mine	③ we	④ us	
	⑤ you	⑥ yours	⑦ your		
	① ➡ Yes, I am joyful. / No, I am not joyful.		② ➡ Yes, I trust you. / No, I don't trust you.		
	③ ➡ My favorite color is red.		④ ➡ This is our plan.		
	⑤ ➡ Katy bought yours.				

| UNIT 4 p.99 | 1. he | 2. They | 3. his | 4. his | 5. theirs |
| Activity | 1. her / hers | 2. her / him | 3. It / Its | | |

| Exercise 1 p.101 | 1. He | 2. them | 3. Its | 4. hers | 5. him |

| Exercise 2 | 1. His | 2. them | 3. hers | 4. he | 5. It |

| Sentence Completion p.102 | 1. (A) | 2. (A) | 3. (A) | 4. (C) | 5. (A) | 6. (D) | 7. (B) | 8. (D) | 9. (D) | 10. (A) |

Unit Review p.106	1. ① his	② him	③ hers		
	④ it	⑤ they	⑥ them		
	① ➡ She is eating a loaf of bread.		② ➡ Her birthday is May 1st.		
	③ ➡ It is under the table.		④ ➡ They are in the living room.		
	⑤ ➡ He is my friend.				

| TOSEL 실전문제 2 | 1. (C) | 2. (D) | 3. (D) | 4. (B) | 5. (C) | 6. (B) | 7. (D) | 8. (B) | 9. (C) | 10. (C) |
| | 11. (D) | 12. (D) | 13. (C) | 14. (C) | 15. (B) | 16. (C) | 17. (B) | 18. (D) | 19. (C) | 20. (C) |

UNIT 1 p.115	1. am	2. are, were	3. has	4. are, were
Activity	1. are, were, have	2. am, was, have	3. are, were, have
	4. was, has, is	5. was, has, is	6. are, were, have

Exercise 1 p.117	1. I	2. is	3. loves	4. We	5. declare				
Exercise 2	1. stop	2. is	3. like	4. drives	5. finishes				
Sentence Completion p.118	1. (A)	2. (B)	3. (D)	4. (A)	5. (C)	6. (B)	7. (D)	8. (C)	9. (A) 10. (B)

Unit Review p.122
1. ➡ She has big eyes.
2. ➡ We were touched.
3. ➡ They are going to take a bus.
4. ➡ I was playing soccer game.

UNIT 2 p.125
1. went　　2. kept　　3. came　　4. put　　5. bought

Activity
1. cut　　2. Let　　3. put
4. cost　　5. hit　　6. hurt

Exercise 1 p.127	1. cut	2. ate	3. bought	4. gave	5. heard				
Exercise 2	1. caught	2. began	3. lost	4. left	5. put				
Sentence Completion p.128	1. (C)	2. (B)	3. (B)	4. (D)	5. (A)	6. (B)	7. (C)	8. (A)	9. (B) 10. (A)

Unit Review p.132
1. ❶ ➡ My friend became an actor.　　❷ ➡ Peter came home early.
　 ❸ ➡ I took a bus today morning.　　❹ ➡ I met my cousin yesterday.
2. ❶ ➡ He put the cushion on the chair.　　❷ ➡ I cut it with a knife.
　 ❸ ➡ It cost thirty dollars.　　❹ ➡ Diana hurt my feelings.

UNIT 3 p.135
1. am not　　2. does not have　　3. did　　4. was

Activity
(O) 1, 3, 4　　(X) 2, 5, 6

Exercise 1 p.137	1. is not	2. was	3. don't	4. is not	5. didn't				
Exercise 2	1. is	2. have	3. is	4. go	5. were				
Sentence Completion p.138	1. (D)	2. (C)	3. (A)	4. (A)	5. (A)	6. (A)	7. (A)	8. (A)	9. (C) 10. (D)

Unit Review p.142
1. ❶ ➡ He is not[isn't] our enemy.　　❷ ➡ We were in the library.
2. ❶ ➡ It does not[doesn't] matter.　　❷ ➡ I didn't fix the computer.
3. ❶ ➡ She doesn't have a note.　　❷ ➡ They didn't have identity cards.

UNIT 4 p.145
1. would　　2. could　　3. might　　4. had to

Activity
1. could　　2. would　　3. might

Exercise 1 p.147	1. go	2. Can	3. had to	4. borrow	5. will not				
Exercise 2	1. should	2. can	3. will	4. Can	5. will				
Sentence Completion p.148	1. (A)	2. (A)	3. (B)	4. (B)	5. (C)	6. (B)	7. (A)	8. (A)	9. (B) 10. (D)

Unit Review p.152
1. ❶ would　　❷ will not [won't]　　❸ would not [wouldn't]
　 ❶ ➡ Will[Would] you read a book for me?
2. ❶ could　　❷ can not [can't]　　❸ could not [couldn't]
　 ❶ ➡ She can not[can't] fail the exam.
3. ❶ might　　❷ may not [mayn't]　　❸ might not [mightn't]
　 ❶ ➡ You may sit on the sofa.
4. ❶ have to　　❷ had to　　❸ must not
　 ❶ ➡ You had to submit your report.

TOSEL 실전문제 3

1. (C)	2. (B)	3. (A)	4. (B)	5. (A)	6. (A)	7. (C)	8. (C)	9. (C)	10. (B)
11. (A)	12. (D)	13. (B)	14. (C)	15. (D)	16. (D)	17. (A)	18. (D)	19. (A)	20. (D)

MEMO

MEMO

MEMO